THE SECOND 100 CHINESE CHARACTERS

SIMPLIFIED CHARACTER EDITION

The Quick and Easy Method to Learn
the second 100 Basic Chinese Characters

Introduction by
Alison and Lawrence Matthews

TUTTLE PUBLISHING
Tokyo • Rutland, Vermont • Singapore

Published by Tuttle Publishing, an imprint of Periplus Editions (HK) Ltd, with editorial offices at 364 Innovation Drive, North Clarendon, Vermont 05759 and 130 Joo Seng Road, #06-01, Singapore 368357.

ISBN-10: 0-8048-3831-3
ISBN-13: 978-0-8048-3831-3

Distributed by:

Japan
Tuttle Publishing
Yaekari Building 3F
5-4-12 Osaki, Shinagawa-ku
Tokyo 141-0032, Japan
Tel: (03) 5437 0171
Fax: (03) 5437 0755
Email: tuttle-sales@gol.com

North America, Latin America & Europe
Tuttle Publishing
364 Innovation Drive
North Clarendon, VT 05759-9436
Tel: (802) 773 8930
Fax: (802) 773 6993
Email: info@tuttlepublishing.com
www.tuttlepublishing.com

Asia-Pacific
Berkeley Books Pte Ltd
130 Joo Seng Road, 06-01/03
Singapore 368357
Tel: (65) 6280 1330
Fax: (65) 6280 6290
Email: inquiries@periplus.com.sg
www.periplus.com

Indonesia
PT Java Books Indonesia
Kawasan Industri Pulogadung
Jl. Rawa Gelam IV No. 9
Jakarta 13930, Indonesia
Telp. (021) 4682 1088
Fax. (021) 461 0207
Email: cs@javabooks.co.id

09 08 07 06
8 7 6 5 4 3 2 1

Printed in Singapore

Contents

Introduction

Learning the characters is one of the most fascinating and fun parts of learning Chinese, and people are often surprised by how much they enjoy being able to recognize them and to write them. Added to that, *writing* the characters is also the best way of *learning* them. This book shows you how to write the second 100 most common characters and gives you plenty of space to practice writing them. When you do this, you'll be learning a writing system which is one of the oldest in the world and is now used by more than a billion people around the globe every day.

In this introduction we'll talk about:
- how the characters developed;
- the difference between traditional and simplified forms of the characters;
- what the "radicals" are and why they're useful;
- how to count the writing strokes used to form each character;
- how to look up the characters in a dictionary;
- how words are created by joining two characters together; and, most importantly;
- how to write the characters!

Also, in case you're using this book on your own without a teacher, we'll tell you how to get the most out of using it.

Chinese characters are not nearly as strange and complicated as people seem to think. They're actually no more mysterious than musical notation, which most people can master in only a few months. So there's really nothing to be scared of or worried about: everyone can learn them—it just requires a bit of patience and perseverance. There are also some things which you may have heard about writing Chinese characters that aren't true. In particular, you don't need to use a special brush to write them (a ball-point pen is fine), and you don't need to be good at drawing (in fact you don't even need to have neat handwriting, although it helps!).

How many characters are there?

Thousands! You would probably need to know something like two thousand to be able to read Chinese newspapers and books, but you don't need anything like that number to read a menu, go shopping or read simple street signs and instructions. Just as you can get by in most countries knowing about a hundred words of the local language, so too you can get by in China quite well knowing a hundred common Chinese characters. And this would also be an excellent basis for learning to read and write Chinese.

How did the characters originally develop?

Chinese characters started out as pictures representing simple objects, and the first characters originally resembled the things they represented. For example:

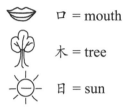

口 = mouth

木 = tree

日 = sun

Some other simple characters were pictures of "ideas":

一 one   二 two   三 three

Some of these characters kept this "pictographic" or "ideographic" quality about them, but others were gradually modified or abbreviated until many of them now look nothing like the original objects or ideas.

Then, as words were needed for things which weren't easy to draw, existing characters were "combined" to create new characters. For example, 女 (meaning "woman") combined with 子 (meaning "child") gives a new character 好 (which means "good" or "to be fond of").

Notice that when two characters are joined together like this to form a new character, they get squashed together and deformed slightly. This is so that the new, combined character will fit into the same size square or "box" as each of the original two characters. For example the character 日 "sun" becomes thinner when it is the left-hand part of the character 时 "time"; and it becomes shorter when it is the upper part of the character 星 "star". Some components got distorted and deformed even more than this in the combining process: for example when the character 人 "man" appears on the left-hand side of a complex character it gets compressed into 亻, like in the character 他 "he".

So you can see that some of the simpler characters often act as basic "building blocks" from which more complex characters are formed. This means that if you learn how to write these simple characters you'll also be learning how to write some complex ones too.

How are characters read and pronounced?

The pronunciations in this workbook refer to modern standard Chinese. This is the official language of China and is also known as "Mandarin" or "**putonghua**".

The pronunciation of Chinese characters is written out with letters of the alphabet using a romanization system called "Hanyu Pinyin"—or "**pinyin**" for short. This is the modern system used in China. In pinyin some of the letters have a different sound than in English— but if you are learning Chinese you'll already know this. We could give a description here of how to pronounce each sound, but it would take up a lot of space—and this workbook is about writing the characters, not pronouncing them! In any case, you really need to hear a teacher (or recording) pronounce the sounds out loud to get an accurate idea of what they sound like.

Each Chinese character is pronounced using only one syllable. However, in addition to the syllable, each character also has a particular *tone*, which refers to how the pitch of the voice is used. In standard Chinese there are four different tones, and in pinyin the tone is marked by placing an accent mark over the vowel as follows:

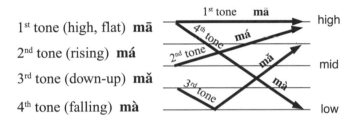

1st tone (high, flat) **mā**

2nd tone (rising) **má**

3rd tone (down-up) **mǎ**

4th tone (falling) **mà**

The pronunciation of each character is therefore a combination of a syllable and a tone. There are only a small number of available syllables in Chinese, and many characters therefore share the same syllable—in fact many characters share the same sound plus tone combination. They are like the English words "here" and "hear"—when they are spoken, you can only tell which is which from the context or by seeing the word in written form.

Apart from **putonghua** (modern standard Chinese), another well-known type of Chinese is Cantonese, which is spoken in southern China and in many Chinese communities around the world. In fact there are several dozen different Chinese languages, and the pronunciations of Chinese characters in these languages are all very different from each other. But the important thing to realize is that the characters themselves do *not* change. So two Chinese people who can't understand each other when they're talking together, can write to one another without any problem at all!

Simplified and traditional characters

As more and more characters were introduced over the years by combining existing characters, some of them became quite complicated. Writing them required many strokes which was time-consuming, and it became difficult to distinguish some of them, especially when the writing was small. So when writing the characters quickly in hand-written form, many people developed short-cuts and wrote them in a more simplified form. In the middle of the 20th century, the Chinese decided to create a standardised set of simplified characters to be used by everyone in China. This resulted in many of the more complicated characters being given simplified forms, making them much easier to learn and to write. Today in China, and also in Singapore, these simplified characters are used almost exclusively, and many Chinese no longer learn the old traditional forms. However the full traditional forms continue to be used in Taiwan and in overseas Chinese communities around the world.

Here are some examples of how some characters were simplified:

Traditional		**Simplified**
見	→	见
飯	→	饭
號	→	号
幾	→	几

Modern standard Chinese uses only simplified characters. But it is useful to be able to recognize the traditional forms as they are still used in many places outside China, and of course older books and inscriptions were also written using the traditional forms. This workbook teaches the full simplified forms. If there is a traditional form, then it is shown in a separate box on the right-hand side of the page so that you can see what it looks like. Where there is no traditional form, the character was considered simple enough already and was left unchanged.

How is Chinese written?

Chinese was traditionally written from top to bottom in columns beginning on the right-hand side of the page and working towards the left, like this:

幸福一点儿也不
难拥有。只要你
常为人着想，带
来欢乐，你会发
觉到那也是一种
幸福呀！

This means that for a book printed in this way, you start by opening it at (what Westerners would think of as) the back cover. While writing in columns is sometimes considered archaic, you will still find many books, especially novels and more serious works of history, printed in this way.

Nowadays, though, most Chinese people write from left to right in horizontal lines working from the top of a page to the bottom, just as we do in English.

Are Chinese characters the same as English words?

Although each character has a meaning, it's not really true that an individual character is equivalent to an English "word". Each character is actually only a single *syllable*. In Chinese (like in English) some words are just one syllable, but most words are made up of two or more syllables joined together. The vast majority of words in Chinese actually consist of two separate characters placed together in a pair. These multi-syllable words are often referred to as "compounds", and this workbook provides a list of common compounds for each character.

Some Chinese characters are one-syllable words on their own (like the English words "if" and "you"), while other characters are only ever used as one half of a word (like the English syllables "sen" and "tence"). Some characters do both: they're like the English "light" which is happy as a word on its own, but which also links up to form words like "headlight" or "lighthouse".

The Chinese write sentences by stringing characters together in a long line from left to right (or in a column from top to bottom), with equal-sized spaces between each character. If English were written this way—as individual syllables rather than as words that are joined together—it would mean all the syllables would be written separately with spaces in between them, something like this:

If you can un der stand this sen tence you can read Chi nese too.

So in theory, you can't see which characters are paired together to form words, but in practice, once you know a bit of Chinese, you can!

Punctuation was not traditionally used when writing Chinese, but today commas, periods (full stops), quotation marks, and exclamation points are all used along with other types of punctuation which have been borrowed from English.

Two ways of putting characters together

We have looked at *combining characters* together to make new *characters*, and *pairing characters* together to make *words*. So what's the difference?

Well, when two *simple characters* are combined to form a new *complex character*, they are squashed or distorted so that the new character fits into the same size square as the original characters. The meaning of the new character *may* be related to the meaning of its components, but it frequently appears to have no connection with them at all! The new complex character also has a new single-syllable pronunciation, which may or may not be related to the pronunciation of one of its parts. For example:

女		也		她
nǚ	+	**yě**	=	**tā**
woman		also		she

日		月		明
rì	+	**yuè**	=	**míng**
sun		moon/month		bright

On the other hand, when characters are *paired together* to create *words*, the characters are simply written one after the other, normal sized, with a normal space in between (and there are no hyphens or anything to show that these characters are working together as a pair). The resulting word has a pronunciation which is *two* syllables—it is simply the pronunciations of the two individual characters one after the other. Also, you're much more likely to be able to guess the meaning of the word from the meanings of the individual characters that make it up. For example:

大		人		大人
dà	+	**rén**	=	**dà rén**
big		person		adult

姐		妹		姐妹
jiě	+	**mèi**	=	**jiě mèi**
older sister		younger sister		sisters

四		月		四月
sì	+	**yuè**	=	**sì yuè**
four		moon/month		April

再		见		再见
zài	+	**jiàn**	=	**zài jiàn**
again		see; meet		Goodbye!

Is it necessary to learn words as well as characters?
As we've said, the meaning of a compound word is often related to the meanings of the individual characters. But this is not always the case, and sometimes the word takes on a new and very specific meaning. So to be able to read Chinese sentences and understand what they mean, it isn't enough just to learn individual character—you'll also need to learn words. (In fact, many individual characters have very little meaning at all by themselves, and only take on meanings when paired with other characters).

Here are some examples of common Chinese words where the meaning of the overall word is not what you might expect from the meanings of the individual characters:

明		天		明天
míng	$+$	**tiān**	$=$	**míng tiān**
bright		day/sky		tomorrow

好		在		好在
hǎo	$+$	**zài**	$=$	**hǎo zài**
good		be present at/		fortunately
		live at		

If you think about it, the same thing happens in English. If you know what "battle" and "ship" mean, you can probably guess what a "battleship" might be. But this wouldn't work with "championship"! Similarly, you'd be unlikely to guess the meaning of "honeymoon" if you only knew the words "honey" and "moon".

The good news is that learning compound words can help you to learn the characters. For example, you may know (from your Chinese lessons) that **xīng qī** means "week". So when you see that this word is written 星期, you will know that 星 is pronounced **xīng**, and 期 is pronounced **qī**—even when these characters are forming part of *other* words. In fact, you will find that you remember many characters as half of some familiar word.

When you see a word written in characters, you can also often see how the word came to mean what it does. For example, **xīng qī** is 星期 which literally means "star period". This will help you to remember both the word *and* the two individual characters.

What is a stroke count?
Each Chinese character is made up of a number of pen or brush strokes. Each individual stroke is the mark made by a pen or brush before lifting it off the paper to write the next stroke. Strokes come in various shapes and sizes—a stroke can be a straight line, a curve, a bent line, a line

with a hook, or a dot. There is a traditional and very specific way that every character should be written. The order and direction of the strokes are both important if the character is to have the correct appearance.

What counts as a stroke is determined by tradition and is not always obvious. For example, the small box that often appears as part of a character (like the one on page 94, in the character 口) counts as three strokes, not four! (This is because a single stroke is traditionally used to write the top and right-hand sides of the box).

All this may sound rather pedantic but it is well worth learning how to write the characters correctly and with the correct number of strokes. One reason is that knowing how to count the strokes correctly is useful for looking up characters in dictionaries, as you'll see later.

This book shows you how to write characters stroke by stroke, and once you get the feel of it you'll very quickly learn how to work out the stroke count of a character you haven't met before, and get it right!

What are radicals?
Although the earliest characters were simple drawings, most characters are complex with two or more parts. And you'll find that some simple characters appear over and over again as parts of many complex characters. Have a look at these five characters:

> 她 she
> 妈 mother
> 姐 older sister
> 好 good
> 姓 surname

All five of these characters have the same component on the left-hand side: 女, which means "woman". This component gives a clue to the meaning of the character, and is called the "radical". As you can see, most of these five characters have something to do with the idea of "woman", but as you can also see, it's not a totally reliable way of guessing the meaning of a character. (Meanings of characters are something you just have to learn, without much help from their component parts).

Unfortunately the radical isn't always on the left-hand side of a character. Sometimes it's on the right, or on the top, or on the bottom. Here are some examples:

Character	Radical	Position of radical
都	阝	right
星	日	top
您	心	bottom
这	辶	left and bottom

Because it's not always easy to tell what the radical is for a particular character, it's given explicitly in a separate box for each of the characters in this book. However, as you learn more and more characters, you'll find that you can often guess the radical just by looking at a character.

Why bother with radicals? Well, for hundreds of years Chinese dictionaries have used the radical component of each character as a way of indexing them. All characters, even the really simple ones, are assigned to one radical or another so that they can be placed within the index of a Chinese dictionary (see the next section).

Incidentally, when you take away the radical, what's left is often a clue to the *pronunciation* of the character (this remainder is called the "phonetic component"). For example, 吗 and 妈 are formed by adding different radicals to the character 马 "horse" which is pronounced **mǎ**. Now 吗 is pronounced **ma** and 妈 is pronounced **mā**, so you can see that these two characters have inherited their pronunciations from the phonetic component 马. Unfortunately these "phonetic components" aren't very dependable: for example 也 on its own is pronounced **yě** but 他 and 她 are both pronounced **tā**.

How do I find a character in an index or a dictionary?

This is a question lots of people ask, and the answer varies according to the type of dictionary you are using. Many dictionaries today are organized alphabetically by pronunciation. So if you want to look up a character in a dictionary and you know its pronunciation, then it's easy. It's when you don't know the pronunciation of a character that there's a problem, since there is no alphabetical order for characters like there is for English words.

If you don't know the pronunciation of a character, then you will need to use a radical index (which is why radicals are useful). To use this you have to know which part of the character is the radical, and you will also need to be able to count the number of strokes that make up the character. To look up 姓, for example, 女 is the radical (which has 3 strokes) and the remaining part 生 has 5 strokes. So first you find the radical 女 amongst the 3-stroke radicals in the radical index. Then, since there are lots of characters under 女, look for 姓 in the section which lists all the 女 characters which have 5-stroke remainders.

This workbook has both a Hanyu Pinyin index and a radical index. Why not get used to how these indexes work by picking a character in the book and seeing if you can find it in both of the indexes?

Many dictionaries also have a pure stroke count index (i.e. ignoring the radical). This is useful if you cannot figure out what the radical of the character is. To use this you must count up all the strokes in the character as a whole and then look the character up under that number (so you would look up 姓 under 8 strokes). As you can imagine, this type of index can leave you with long columns of characters to scan through before you find the one you're looking for, so it's usually a last resort!

All these methods have their pitfalls and complications, so recently a completely new way of looking up characters has been devised. The *Chinese Character Fast Finder* (see the inside back cover) organizes characters purely by their shapes so that you can look up any one of 3,000 characters very quickly without knowing its meaning, radical, pronunciation or stroke count!

How should I use this workbook?

One good way to learn characters is to practice writing them, especially if you think about what each character means as you write it. This will fix the characters in your memory better than if you just look at them without writing them.

If you're working on your own without a teacher, work on a few characters at a time. Go at a pace that suits you; it's much better to do small but regular amounts of writing than to do large chunks at irregular intervals. You might start with just one or two characters each day and increase this as you get better at it. Frequent repetition is the key! Try to get into a daily routine of learning a few new characters and also reviewing the ones you learned on previous days. It's also a good idea to keep a list of which characters you've learned each day, and then to "test yourself" on the characters you learned the previous day, three days ago, a week ago and a month ago. Each time you test yourself they will stay in your memory for a longer period.

But *don't* worry if you can't remember a character you wrote out ten times only yesterday! This is quite normal to begin with. Just keep going—it will all be sinking in without you realizing it.

Once you've learned a few characters you can use flash cards to test yourself on them in a random order. You can make your own set of cards, or use a ready-made set like *Chinese in a Flash* (see the inside back cover).

How do I write the characters?

Finally, let's get down to business and talk about actually writing the characters! Under each character in this book, the first few boxes show how the character is written, stroke by stroke. There is a correct way to draw each character, and the diagrams in the boxes show you both the order to draw the strokes in, and also the direction for each stroke.

Use the three gray examples to trace over and then carry on by yourself, drawing the characters using the correct stroke order and directions. The varying thicknesses of the lines show you what the characters would look like if they were drawn with a brush, but if you're using a pencil or ball-point pen don't worry about this. Just trace down the middle of the lines and you will produce good hand-written characters.

Pay attention to the length of each of the strokes so that your finished character has the correct proportions. Use the gray dotted lines inside each box as a guide to help you start and end each stroke in the right place.

You may think that it doesn't really matter how the strokes are written as long as the end result looks the same. To some extent this is true, but there are some good reasons for knowing the "proper" way to write the characters. Firstly, it helps you to count strokes, and secondly it will make your finished character "look right", and also help you to read other people's hand-written characters later on. It's better in the long run to learn the correct method of writing the characters from the beginning because, as with so many other things, once you get into "bad" habits it can be very hard to break them!

If you are left-handed, just use your left hand as normal, but still make sure you use the correct stroke order and directions when writing the strokes. For example, draw your horizontal strokes left to right, even if it feels more natural to draw them right to left.

For each Chinese character there is a fixed, correct order in which to write the strokes. But these "stroke orders" do follow some fairly general rules. The main thing to remember is:

- Generally work left to right and top to bottom.

Some other useful guidelines are:
- Horizontal lines are written before vertical ones (see 才, page 52);
- Lines that slope down and to the left are written before those that slope down and to the right (see 分, page 19);
- A central part or vertical line is written before symmetrical or smaller lines at the sides (see 水, page 100);
- The top and sides of an outer box are written first, then whatever is inside the box, then the bottom is written last to "close" it (see 因, page 21).

As you work through the book you'll see these rules in action and get a feel for them, and you'll know how to draw virtually any Chinese character without having to be shown.

Practice, practice, practice!
Your first attempts at writing will be awkward, but as with most things you'll get better with practice. That's why there are lots of squares for you to use. And don't be too hard on yourself (we all draw clumsy-looking characters when we start); just give yourself plenty of time and practice. After a while, you'll be able to look back at your early attempts and compare them with your most recent ones, and see just how much you've improved.

After writing the same character a number of times (a row or two at most), move on to another one. Don't fill up the whole page at one sitting! Then, after writing several other characters, come back later and do a few more of the first one. Can you remember the stroke order without having to look at the diagram?

Finally, try writing out sentences, or lines of different characters, on ordinary paper. To begin with you can mark out squares to write in if you want to, but after that simply imagine the squares and try to keep your characters all equally sized and equally spaced.

Have fun, and remember—the more you practice writing the characters the easier it gets!

岁	**common words**	**6 strokes**
	岁月　**suì yuè**　years 岁数　**suì shu**　age 几岁(?)　**jǐ suì**　how old(?) 同岁　**tóng suì**　same age 周岁　**zhōu suì**　first birthday; one year old	**radical** 夕 **traditional form** 歲
suì years old		

怎

zěn how(?); why(?)

common words

怎么(?) **zěn me** how(?); why(?)
怎么样(?) **zěn me yàng** how about it(?)
怎样(?) **zěn yàng** how about it(?)
怎么回事(?) **zěn me huí shì** what's going on(?)
怎么得了 **zěn me dé liǎo** express a serious condition
不怎么 **bù zěn me** not very

ノ	乍	个	乍	乍	乍	怎	怎
怎	怎	怎	怎				

样

yàng 1. appearance
2. type

common words

样子 **yàng zi** look; appearance
样本 **yàng běn** sample book
一样／同样 **yī yàng/tóng yàng** alike
花样 **huā yàng** 1. variety 2. trick
两样／不一样 **liǎng yàng/bù yī yàng** different
这样 **zhè yàng** in this way

10 strokes

radical

木

traditional form

樣

一	十	才	木	术	术	样	样
样	样	样	样	样			

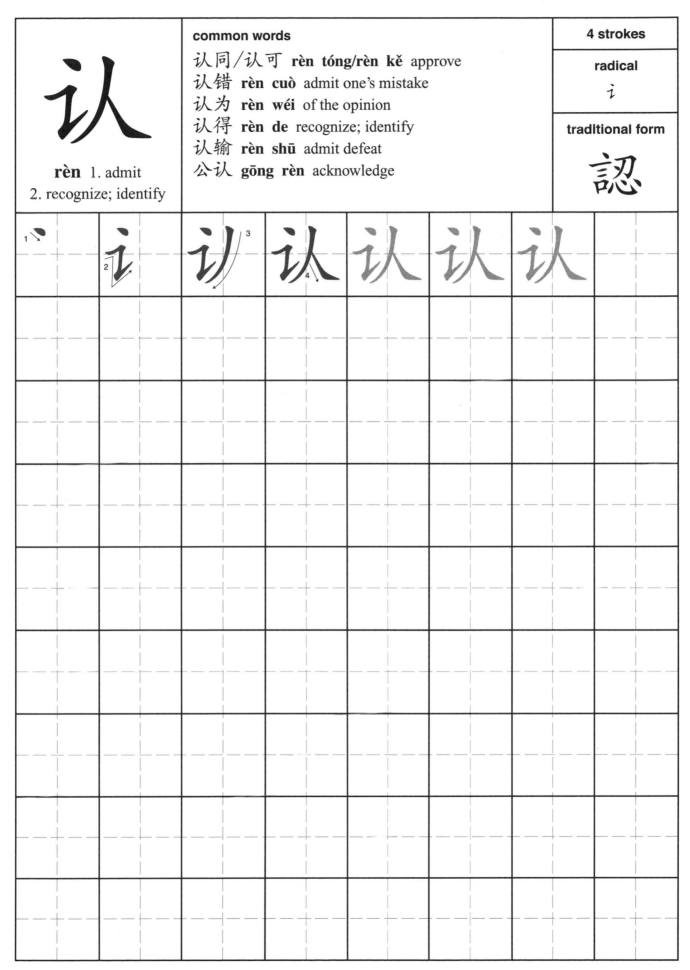

认

rèn 1. admit
2. recognize; identify

common words

认同／认可 **rèn tóng/rèn kě** approve
认错 **rèn cuò** admit one's mistake
认为 **rèn wéi** of the opinion
认得 **rèn de** recognize; identify
认输 **rèn shū** admit defeat
公认 **gōng rèn** acknowledge

4 strokes

radical

讠

traditional form

認

识		7 strokes

shí 1. know; knowledge 2. recognize

common words

识字 **shí zì** literate
识别 **shí bié** distinguish; discern
认识 **rèn shi** know each other
知识 **zhī shi** knowledge
常识 **cháng shí** 1. general knowledge 2. common sense

radical

讠

traditional form

識

现

xiàn present; now

common words

现在 **xiàn zài** now; at present
现金 **xiàn jīn** cash
现场 **xiàn chǎng** scene (of happenings)
现成 **xiàn chéng** readymade
表现 **biǎo xiàn** performance
出现 **chū xiàn** appear

8 strokes

radical

王

traditional form

現

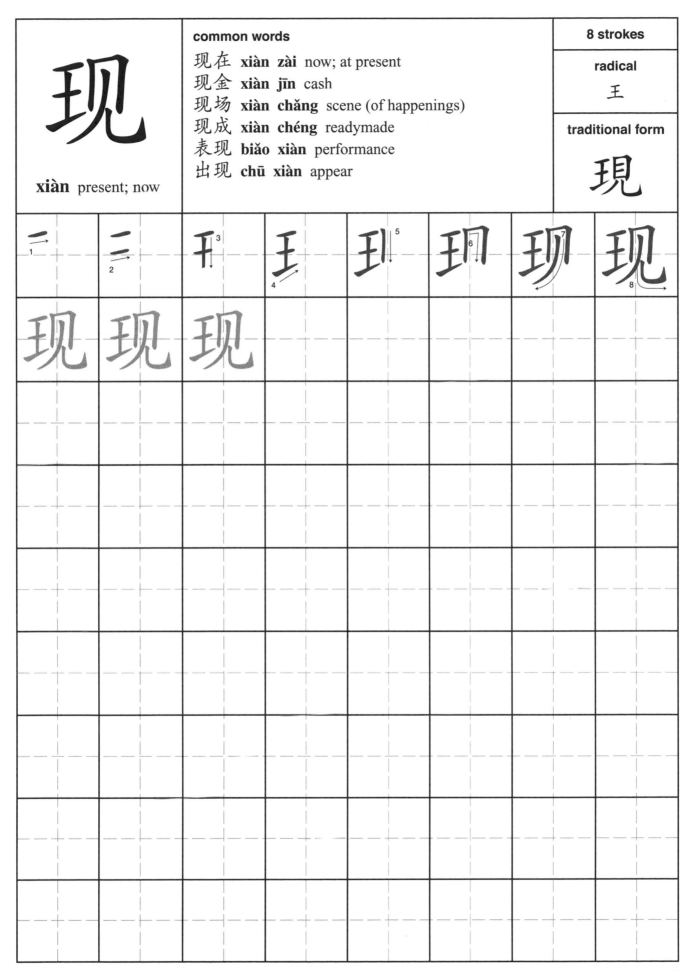

可

kě can; permitted

common words

可以 **kě yǐ** can; permitted
可是 **kě shì** 1. really 2. but
可能 **kě néng** maybe; possible
可口 **kě kǒu** tasty; delicious
可见 **kě jiàn** obviously
可笑 **kě xiào** laughable; funny
还可以 **hái kě yǐ** not bad; all right

5 strokes

radical

口

一　丁　可　可　可　可　可　可

点	common words	9 strokes

点头 **diǎn tóu** nod
点心 **diǎn xīn** snack
点菜 **diǎn cài** order dishes (from a menu)
一点儿／点儿 **yī diǎnr/diǎnr** a little; a bit
三点／三点钟 **sān diǎn/sān diǎn zhōng** three o'clock
雨点 **yǔ diǎn** raindrops
要点 **yào diǎn** main point; essential point

diǎn 1. o'clock
2. dot; drop 3. point

radical
卜

traditional form
點

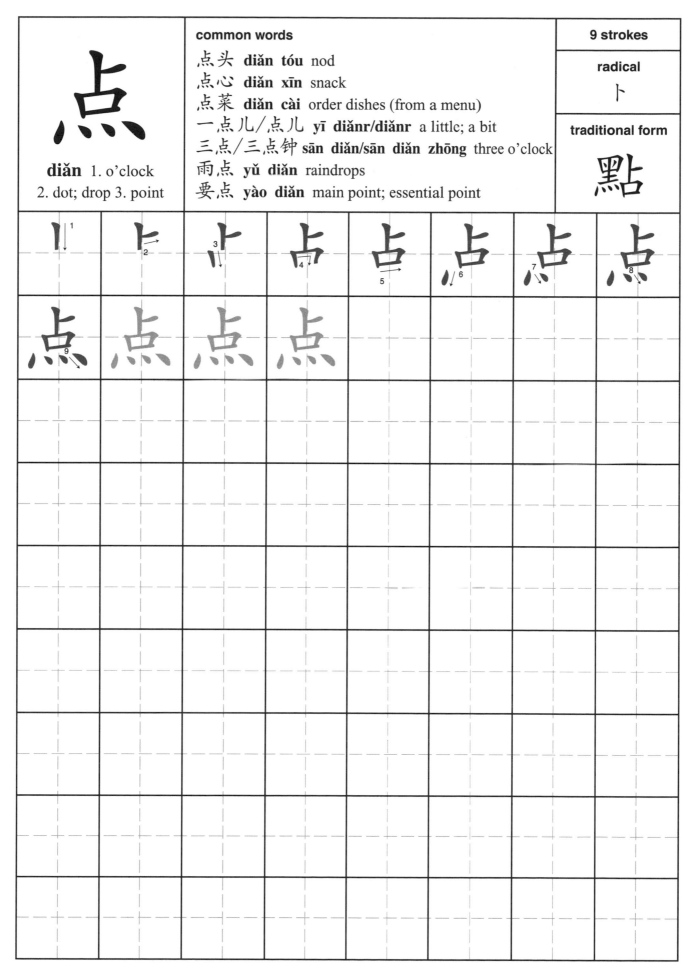

半	**common words**	**5 strokes**
	半天　**bàn tiān**　1. half day 2. a long time	**radical**
bàn　1. half; mid	半价　**bàn jià**　half price	
2. very little/few	半空　**bàn kōng**　in the sky; mid air	`
	九点半　**jiǔ diǎn bàn**　half past nine	
	大半/多半　**dà bàn/duō bàn**　majority	
	另一半　**lìng yī bàn**　other half (of a couple)	

丶	丷	半	半	半	半	半	半

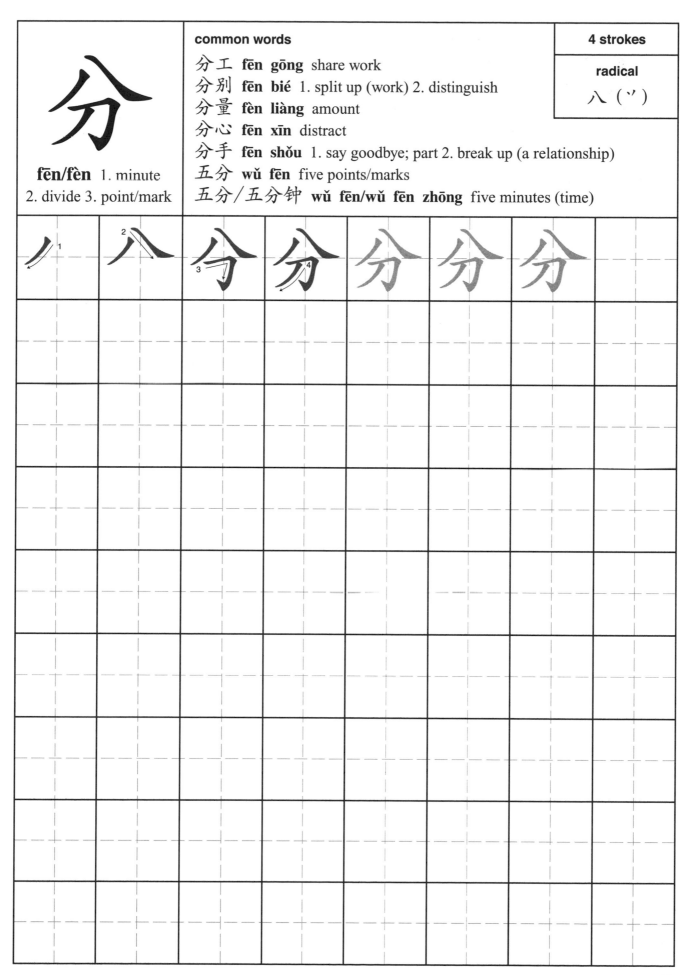

分

fēn/fèn 1. minute
2. divide 3. point/mark

common words

分工 **fēn gōng** share work
分别 **fēn bié** 1. split up (work) 2. distinguish
分量 **fèn liàng** amount
分心 **fēn xīn** distract
分手 **fēn shǒu** 1. say goodbye; part 2. break up (a relationship)
五分 **wǔ fēn** five points/marks
五分/五分钟 **wǔ fēn/wǔ fēn zhōng** five minutes (time)

4 strokes

radical

八 （丷）

19

钟

zhōng 1. bell 2. clock
3. time (measure)

common words

钟声 **zhōng shēng** ringing (of bells)
钟头 **zhōng tóu** hour (time)
钟表 **zhōng biǎo** clocks and watches; timepiece
钟情 **zhōng qíng** deeply in love
分钟 **fēn zhōng** minute (time)

9 strokes

radical

钅

traditional form

鐘

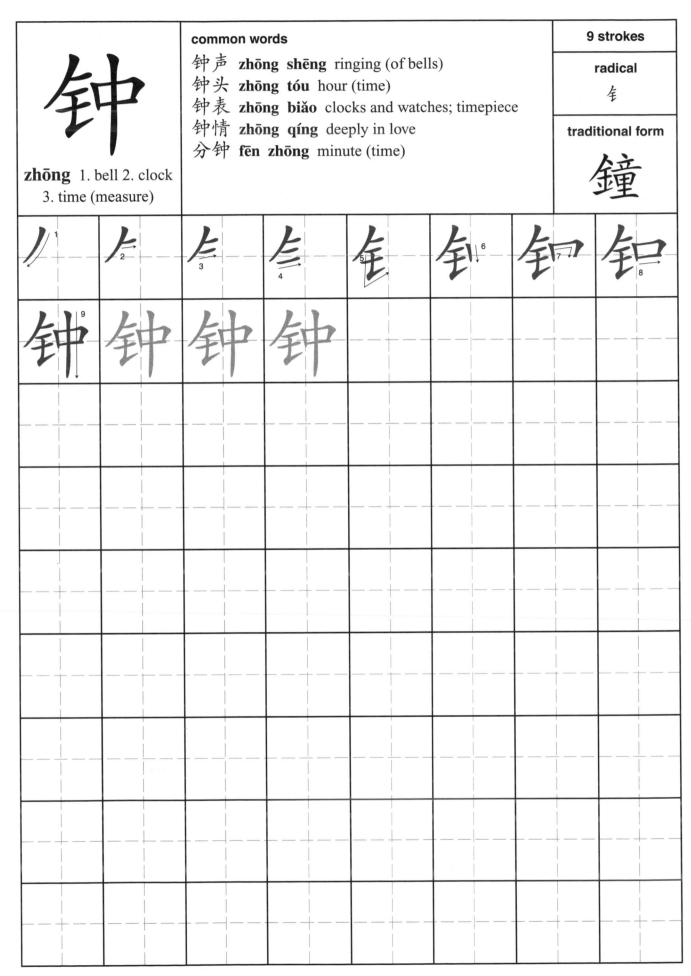

因

yīn because (of);
cause; reason

common words

因此　**yīn cǐ**　so; therefore
因为　**yīn wèi**　because (of)
因而　**yīn ér**　thus; as a result
原因　**yuán yīn**　reason
起因　**qǐ yīn**　cause; origin

为

wèi/wéi 1. for; on behalf of 2. do; act as

radical

、

traditional form

為

common words

为了　**wèi le** in order to; for
为什么(?)　**wèi shěn me** why(?); reason
为人　**wéi rén** a person's conduct/behavior
为生　**wéi shēng** make a living
为难　**wéi nán** make things difficult (for somebody)
为期　**wéi qī** last for a period
为止　**wéi zhǐ** until ...; up to ...

丶	丿	为	为	为	为	为

common words

很高 **hěn gāo** very tall
很矮 **hěn ǎi** very short (height)
很低 **hěn dī** very low
很长 **hěn cháng** very long
很短 **hěn duǎn** very short (length)
很慢 **hěn màn** very slow
很快 **hěn kuài** very fast

hěn very

9 strokes

radical

彳

忙		common words					6 strokes
		忙着 **máng zhe** busy with something					radical
		忙碌 **máng lù** busy					忄
		忙不忙(?) **máng bu máng** busy(?)					
		太忙了 **tài máng le** too busy					
		大忙人 **dà máng rén** a very busy person					
máng busy		帮忙 **bāng máng** (to) help; help					
		急忙 **jí máng** quickly; hastily					

忄¹	㇒²	忄³	忄⁴	忙⁵	忙⁶	忙	忙
忙							

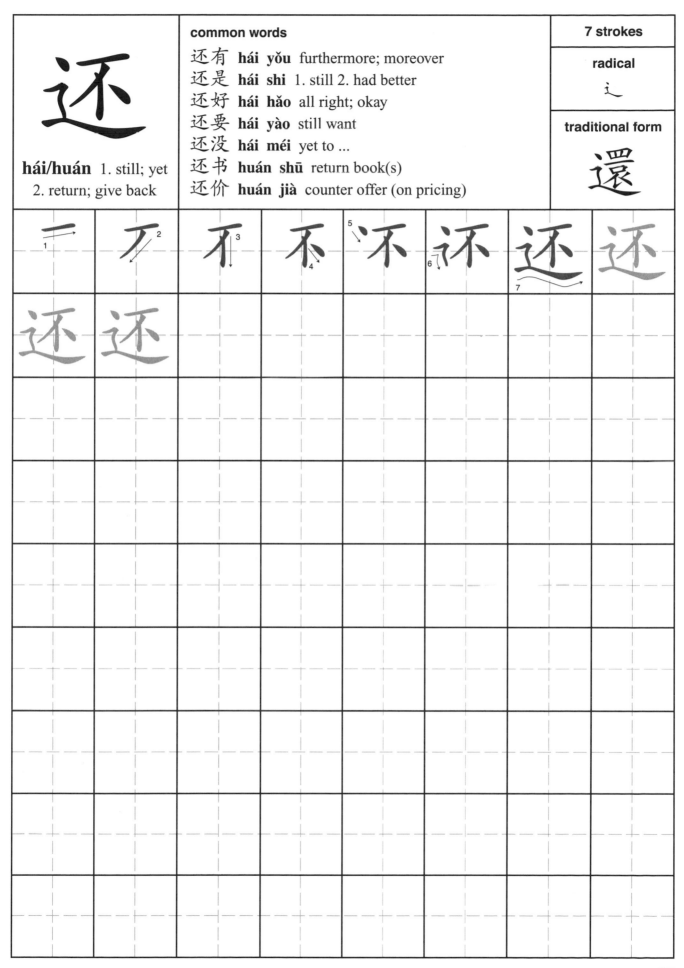

还

hái/huán 1. still; yet
2. return; give back

common words

还有 **hái yǒu** furthermore; moreover
还是 **hái shi** 1. still 2. had better
还好 **hái hǎo** all right; okay
还要 **hái yào** still want
还没 **hái méi** yet to ...
还书 **huán shū** return book(s)
还价 **huán jià** counter offer (on pricing)

7 strokes

radical

辶

traditional form

還

喜

xǐ 1. happy 2. fond of 3. pregnancy

common words

喜欢/喜爱 **xǐ huān/xǐ ài** fond of
喜事 **xǐ shì** happy event
喜酒 **xǐ jiǔ** wedding dinner
恭喜 **gōng xǐ** congratulate
有喜 **yóu xǐ** pregnant
可喜 **kě xǐ** heartening

12 strokes

radical

口

一₁	十²	士₃	吉₄	吉₅	吉₆	吉₇	吉₈
壴₉	喜¹⁰	喜¹¹	喜¹²	喜	喜	喜	

欢

huān 1. happy
2. vigorous

common words

欢乐/欢喜 **huān lè/huān xǐ** happy; joyful
欢迎 **huān yíng** welcome
欢呼 **huān hū** cheer
欢笑 **huān xiào** laugh heartily
欢送 **huān sòng** see ... off
欢心 **huān xīn** favor; fond feeling

6 strokes

radical
又

traditional form
歡

等

děng 1. wait 2. type 3. grade; rank

common words

等候/等待 **děng hòu/děng dài** wait for
等到 **děng dào** wait until; by the time that ...
等等 **děng děng** ... and so on
等于 **děng yú** equals to
上等 **shàng děng** high class
下等 **xià děng** low grade; inferior
平等 **píng děng** equal

12 strokes

radical

⺮

太

tài 1. extremely; too
2. senior

common words

太好了 **tài hǎo le** That's great!
太太 **tài tai** 1. wife 2. Mrs
太子 **tài zi** crown prince
太阳 **tài yáng** sun
太空 **tài kōng** space
太平 **tài píng** peaceful
老太太/老太婆 **lǎo tài tai/lǎo tài pó** old woman

4 strokes

radical

大

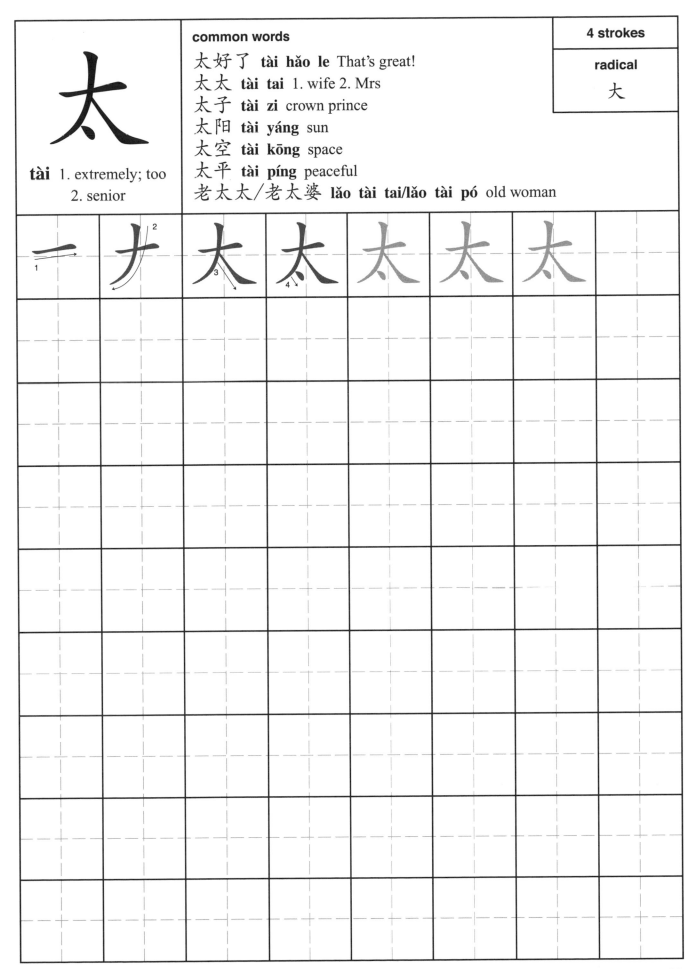

久

jiǔ 1. length of time
2. for a long time

common words

久久 **jiǔ jiǔ** for a very long time
久等 **jiǔ děng** wait for a long time
不久 **bù jiǔ** not a very long time; soon
好久 **hǎo jiǔ** a long time
永久 **yǒng jiǔ** forever; permanent
长久 **cháng jiǔ** for a long time

3 strokes

radical

丿

丿	夕	久	久	久	久		

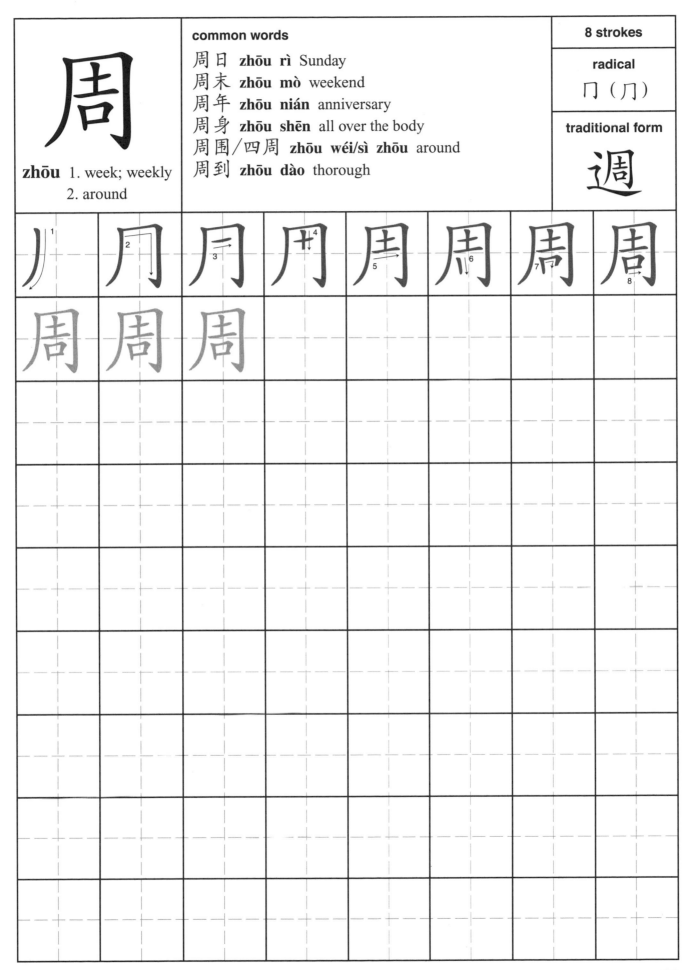

周

zhōu 1. week; weekly
2. around

common words

周日 **zhōu rì** Sunday
周末 **zhōu mò** weekend
周年 **zhōu nián** anniversary
周身 **zhōu shēn** all over the body
周围／四周 **zhōu wéi/sì zhōu** around
周到 **zhōu dào** thorough

8 strokes

radical

冂（几）

traditional form

週

末

mò end; last part

common words

末期 **mò qī** last phase
末日 **mò rì** doomsday
末了 **mò liǎo** last; at the end
末尾 **mò wěi** the end
末班车 **mò bān chē** last train; last bus
周末 **zhōu mò** weekend

5 strokes

radical

一

一　二　丰　才　未　未　未　未

32

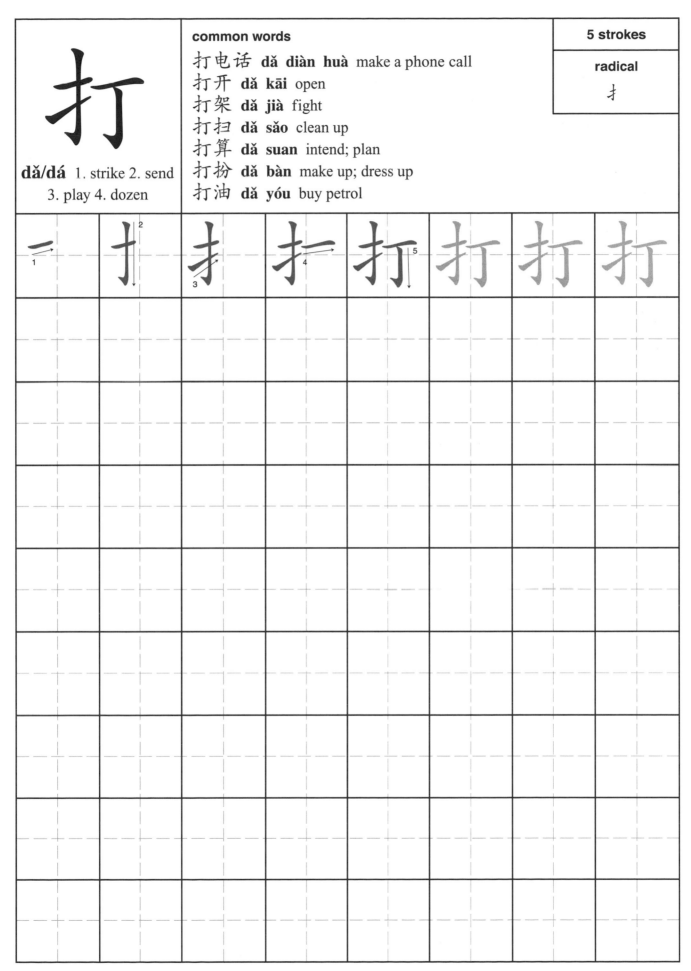

打

dǎ/dá 1. strike 2. send
3. play 4. dozen

common words

打电话 **dǎ diàn huà** make a phone call
打开 **dǎ kāi** open
打架 **dǎ jià** fight
打扫 **dǎ sǎo** clean up
打算 **dǎ suan** intend; plan
打扮 **dǎ bàn** make up; dress up
打油 **dǎ yóu** buy petrol

5 strokes

radical

扌

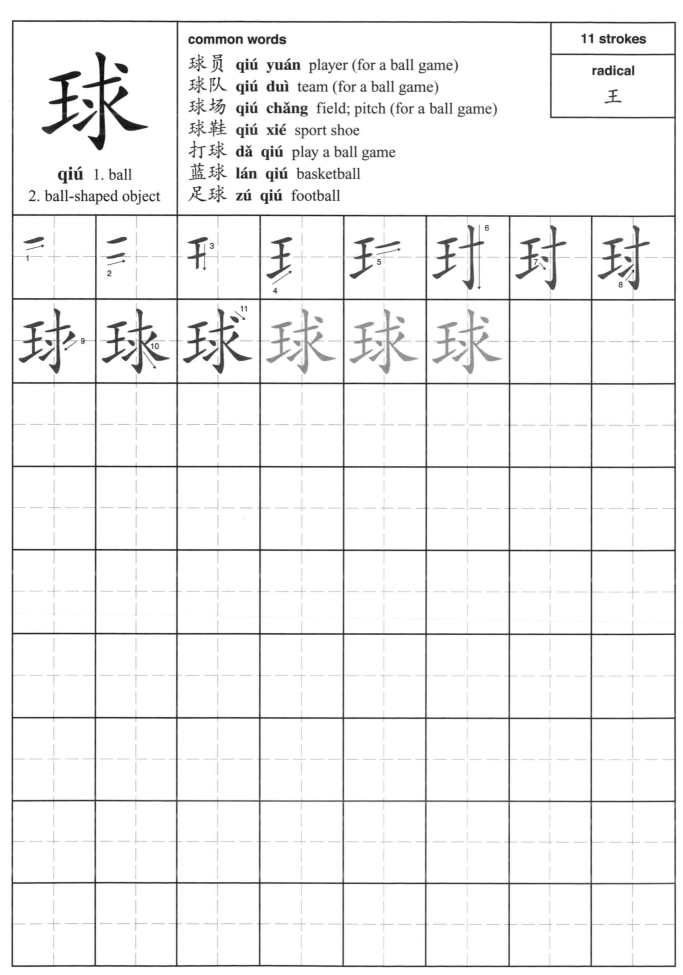

common words

球员	**qiú yuán**	player (for a ball game)
球队	**qiú duì**	team (for a ball game)
球场	**qiú chǎng**	field; pitch (for a ball game)
球鞋	**qiú xié**	sport shoe
打球	**dǎ qiú**	play a ball game
蓝球	**lán qiú**	basketball
足球	**zú qiú**	football

11 strokes

radical

王

qiú 1. ball
2. ball-shaped object

看

kàn/kān 1. see; watch
2. read 3. look after

common words

看看 **kàn kan** have a look
看见 **kàn jiàn** see
看电影 **kàn diàn yǐng** go for a movie
看不起/小看 **kàn bu qǐ/xiǎo kàn** look down on
看病 **kàn bìng** 1. consult a doctor 2. see a patient
看孩子 **kān hái zi** babysit
难看 **nán kàn** ugly; don't look good

9 strokes

radical

目

一	三	三	尹	天	看	看	看
看	看	看	看				

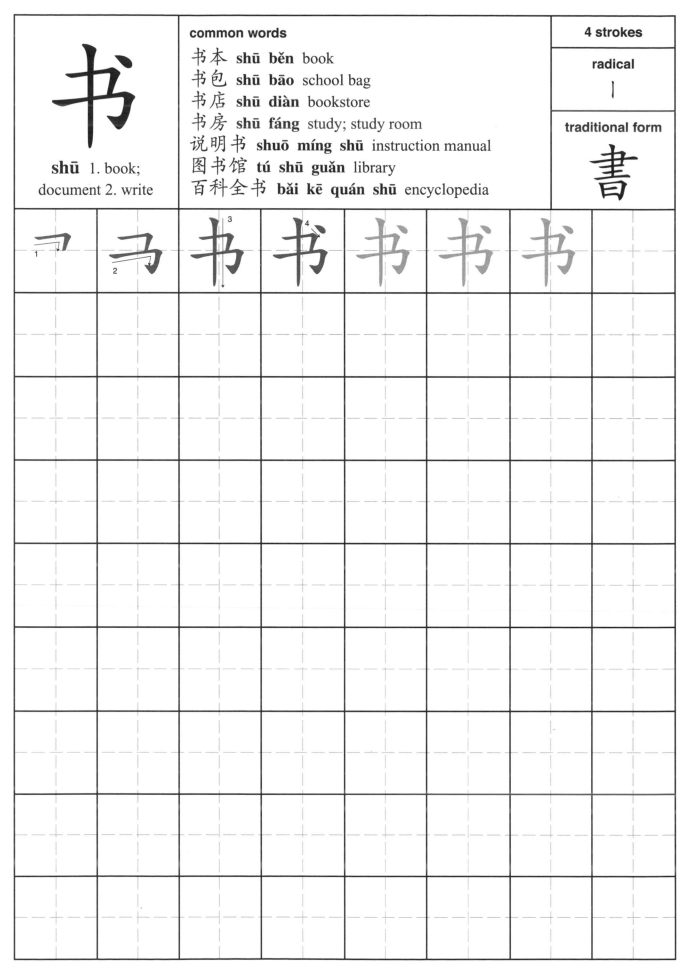

书

shū 1. book; document 2. write

common words

书本 **shū běn** book
书包 **shū bāo** school bag
书店 **shū diàn** bookstore
书房 **shū fáng** study; study room
说明书 **shuō míng shū** instruction manual
图书馆 **tú shū guǎn** library
百科全书 **bǎi kē quán shū** encyclopedia

4 strokes

radical

丨

traditional form

書

常

cháng 1. often
2. common

common words

常常／时常 **cháng cháng/shí cháng** frequently
常见 **cháng jiàn** commonplace; ordinary
常年 **cháng nián** all year round
常人 **cháng rén** ordinary person; man in the street
平常 **píng cháng** ordinary; usual
正常 **zhèng cháng** normal; regular
日常 **rì cháng** everyday; daily

11 strokes

radical

小（⺌）

写

xiě write; compose

common words

写字 **xiě zì** write characters/words
写信 **xiě xìn** write a letter
写作 **xiě zuò** writing; composition
写生 **xiě shēng** sketch/draw from nature
大写 **dà xiě** upper case; write in capital letters
小写 **xiǎo xiě** lower case; write in small letters
填写 **tián xiě** fill out (a form)

radical

冖

traditional form

寫

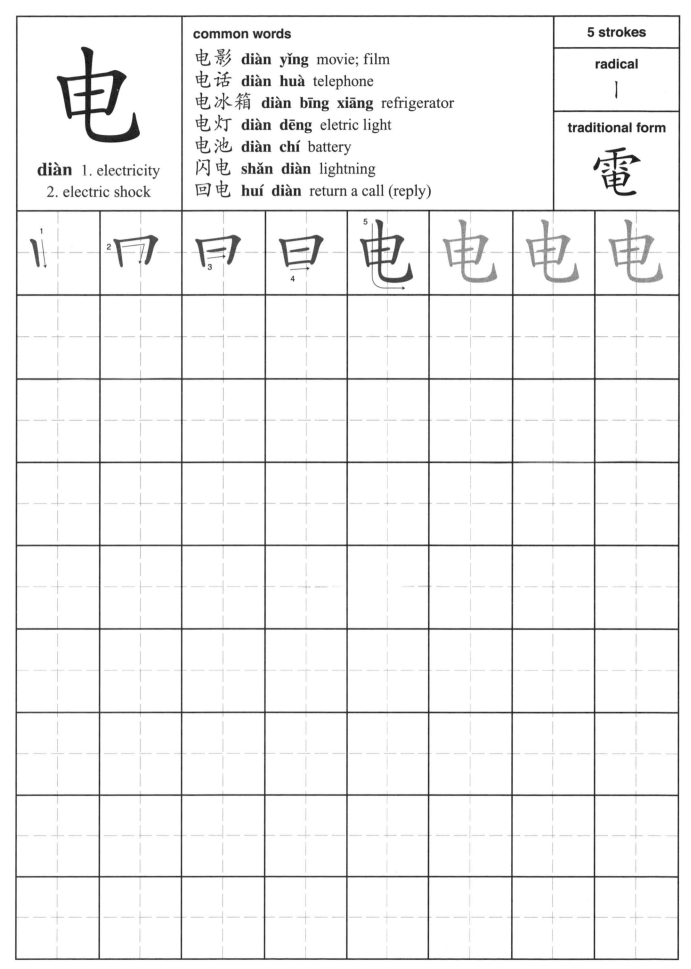

电

diàn 1. electricity
2. electric shock

common words

电影　**diàn yǐng**　movie; film
电话　**diàn huà**　telephone
电冰箱　**diàn bīng xiāng**　refrigerator
电灯　**diàn dēng**　eletric light
电池　**diàn chí**　battery
闪电　**shǎn diàn**　lightning
回电　**huí diàn**　return a call (reply)

5 strokes

radical

丨

traditional form

電

视		**common words**			**8 strokes**
		视力 **shì lì** eyesight; vision			**radical**
		视为 **shì wéi** see as			礻
		电视 **diàn shì** 1. television program 2. television set			
		电视机 **diàn shì jī** television set			**traditional form**
		近视 **jìn shì** myopia; nearsightedness			
shì watch; see		远视 **yuǎn shì** hyperopia; farsightedness			視

丶	礻	礻	礻	礻	视	视	视
视	视	视					

唱

chàng sing

common words

唱歌／歌唱 **chàng gē/gē chàng** sing
唱戏 **chàng xì** sing an opera
唱片 **chàng piàn** record; phonograph
合唱 **hé chàng** sing in chorus
高唱 **gāo chàng** sing loudly
卖唱 **mài chàng** sing for a living; busking

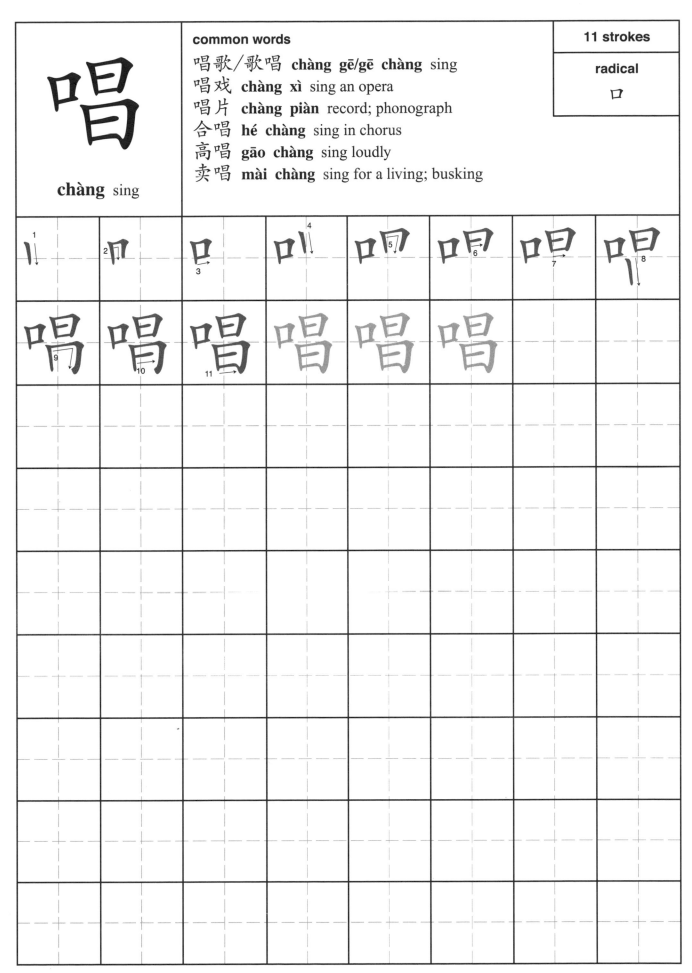

歌

gē song

common words

歌星 **gē xīng** star (singer)
歌手 **gē shǒu** singer; vocalist
歌迷 **gē mí** fan of vocalists
国歌 **guó gē** national anthem
儿歌 **ér gē** nursery rhyme
情歌 **qíng gē** love song

14 strokes

radical

欠

一	丁	口	口	可	叿	哥	哥
哥	哥	哥	歌	歌	歌	歌	歌
歌							

42

吧

ba/bā modal particle

吧台 **bā tái** bar top

酒吧 **jiǔ bā** pub

好吧 **hǎo ba** Okay!; Fine!

走吧 **zǒu ba** Lct's go!

看书吧 **kàn shū ba** Let's read!

再说吧 **zài shuō ba** Let's talk about it later!

7 strokes

radical

口

听	common words	7 strokes
	听见／听到 **tīng jiàn/tīng dào** heard	radical
	听话 **tīng huà** obedient	口
	听写 **tīng xiě** dictate; dictation	
	听说 **tīng shuō** it is said	traditional form
tīng listen; hear	听众 **tīng zhòng** audience; listeners	
	打听 **dǎ tīng** ask; inquire	聽

丨	口	口	叮	听	听	听
听	听					

44

音

yīn sound; tone

common words

音乐 **yīn yuè** music
音乐会 **yīn yuè huì** concert
音乐家 **yīn yuè jiā** musician
声音 **shēng yīn** sound; voice
发音/读音 **fā yīn/dú yīn** pronunciation
口音 **kǒu yīn** accent

9 strokes

radical
音

丶	二	亠	立	立	音	音	音
音	音	音	音				

乐	common words	5 strokes

yuè/lè 1. music 2. happy

common words

乐队 **yuè duì** band; orchestra
乐器 **yuè qì** musical instrument
乐意 **lè yì** wiling to; ready to
乐园 **lè yuán** paradise
快乐 **kuài lè** happy
欢乐 **huān lè** happy; joyful

5 strokes

radical
丿

traditional form
樂

一	二	牙	牙	乐	乐	乐	乐

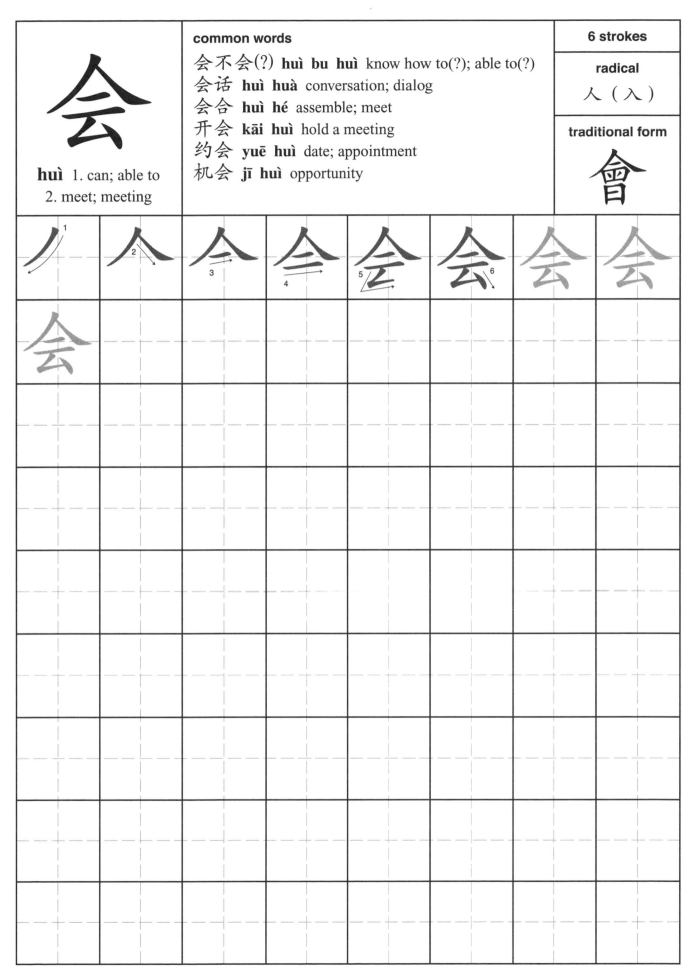

会

huì 1. can; able to
2. meet; meeting

common words

会不会(?) **huì bu huì** know how to(?); able to(?)
会话 **huì huà** conversation; dialog
会合 **huì hé** assemble; meet
开会 **kāi huì** hold a meeting
约会 **yuē huì** date; appointment
机会 **jī huì** opportunity

6 strokes

radical

人（入）

traditional form

會

跳

tiào 1. jump; bounce
2. beat

common words

跳高 **tiào gāo** high jump
跳远 **tiào yuǎn** broad jump
跳水 **tiào shuǐ** dive
跳伞 **tiào sǎn** 1. skydive 2. parachute
跳班 **tiào bān** skip a grade/level
心跳 **xīn tiào** heart palpitation; heartbeat

13 strokes

radical

足（⻊）

丨	口	口	尸	足	⻊	足	趴
趴	趴	跳	跳	跳	跳	跳	跳

48

舞

wǔ dance

common words

舞伴 **wǔ bàn** dancing partner
舞会 **wǔ huì** ball (dance)
舞台 **wǔ tái** stage
跳舞 **tiào wǔ** (to) dance
歌舞 **gē wǔ** song and dance
芭蕾舞 **bā lěi wǔ** ballet

14 strokes

radical

夕

对 duì 1. correct 2. treat 3. compare; check

common words

对不起 **duì bu qǐ** 1. sorry 2. excuse me
对手 **duì shǒu** opponent
对方 **duì fāng** other side; other party
对白 **duì bái** dialog (in a play/film)
不对 **bù duì** 1. wrong 2. odd
反对 **fǎn duì** diagree; against
作对 **zuò duì** oppose

5 strokes

radical

又

traditional form

對

错

cuò mistaken; wrong

common words

错字 **cuò zì** incorrectly written characters/words
错过 **cuò guò** miss (a chance)
不错 **bù cuò** not bad; pretty good
没错 **méi cuò** not wrong; correct
做错 **zuò cuò** do wrongly
写错 **xiě cuò** write wrongly
弄错／搞错 **nòng cuò/gǎo cuò** misunderstand

13 strokes

radical

钅

traditional form

錯

丿	𠂉	乍	钅	钅	钅	钅	钅
错	错	错	错	错	错	错	错

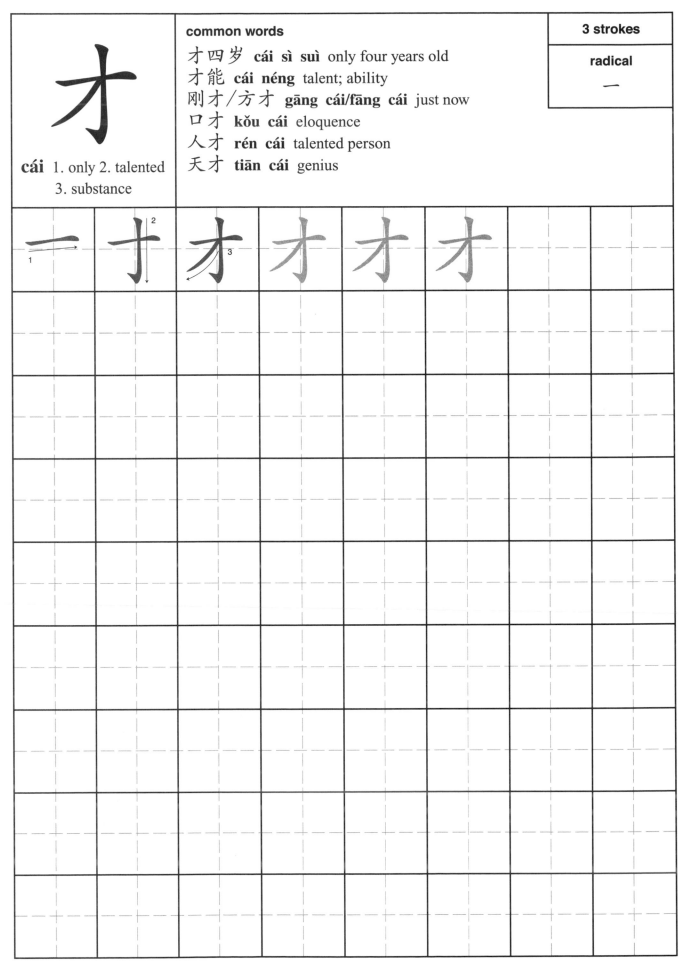

才

cái 1. only 2. talented 3. substance

common words

才四岁 **cái sì suì** only four years old
才能 **cái néng** talent; ability
刚才/方才 **gāng cái/fāng cái** just now
口才 **kǒu cái** eloquence
人才 **rén cái** talented person
天才 **tiān cái** genius

3 strokes

radical

一

一　才　才　才　才　才

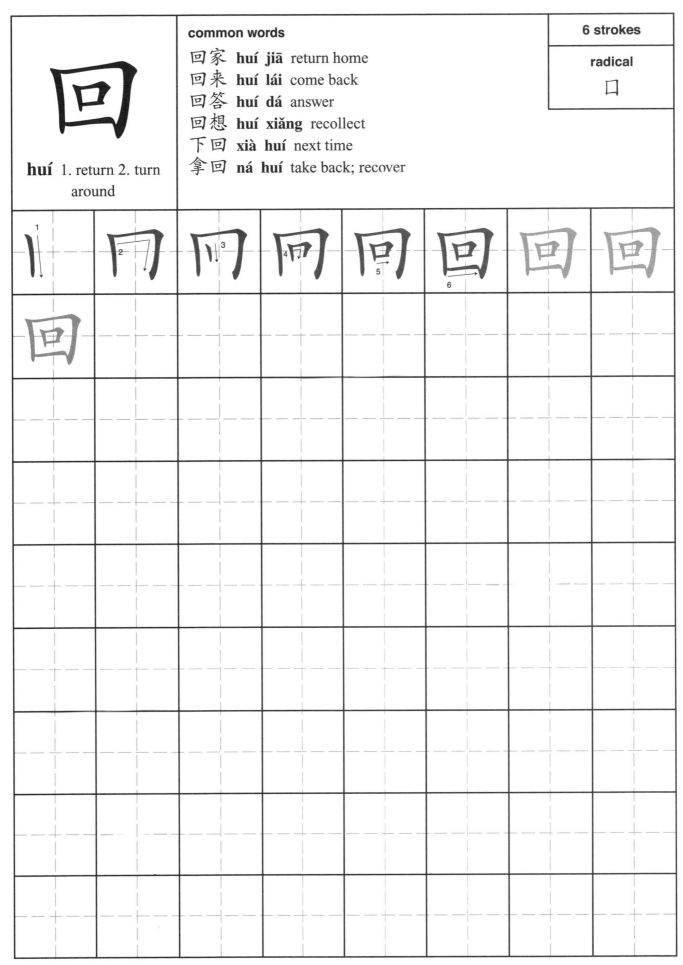

huí 1. return 2. turn around

common words

回家 **huí jiā** return home
回来 **huí lái** come back
回答 **huí dá** answer
回想 **huí xiǎng** recollect
下回 **xià huí** next time
拿回 **ná huí** take back; recover

6 strokes

radical

口

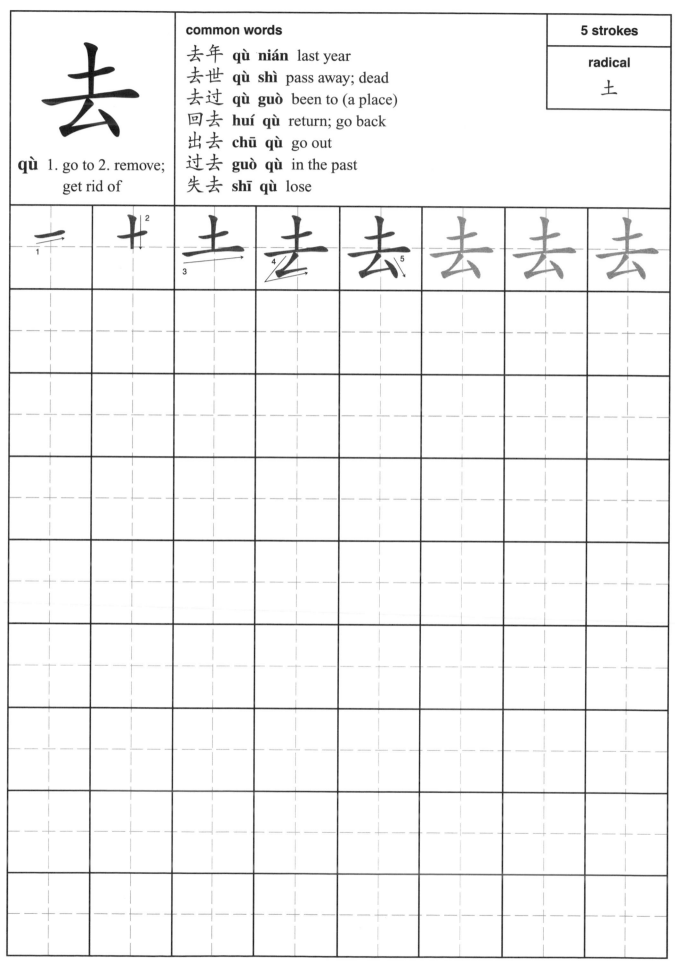

去

qù 1. go to 2. remove; get rid of

common words

去年 **qù nián** last year
去世 **qù shì** pass away; dead
去过 **qù guò** been to (a place)
回去 **huí qù** return; go back
出去 **chū qù** go out
过去 **guò qù** in the past
失去 **shī qù** lose

5 strokes

radical

土

所

suǒ 1. place (location)
2. measure word

common words

所有 **suǒ yǒu** 1. all 2. (one) owns/possesses
所在 **suǒ zài** located; location
厕所 **cè suǒ** toilet; bathroom
住所 **zhù suǒ** residence
诊所 **zhěn suǒ** clinic
两所医院 **liǎng suǒ yī yuàn** two hospitals

8 strokes

radical

斤

以

yǐ 1. use; by means of
2. according to; because

common words

以为 **yǐ wéi** think; believe
以后 **yǐ hòu** afterward; after
以前 **yǐ qián** before; previously
以及 **yǐ jí** and; as well as
以上 **yǐ shàng** above; onward
以外 **yǐ wài** excluding; beyond
所以 **suǒ yǐ** therefore

4 strokes

radical

人（入）

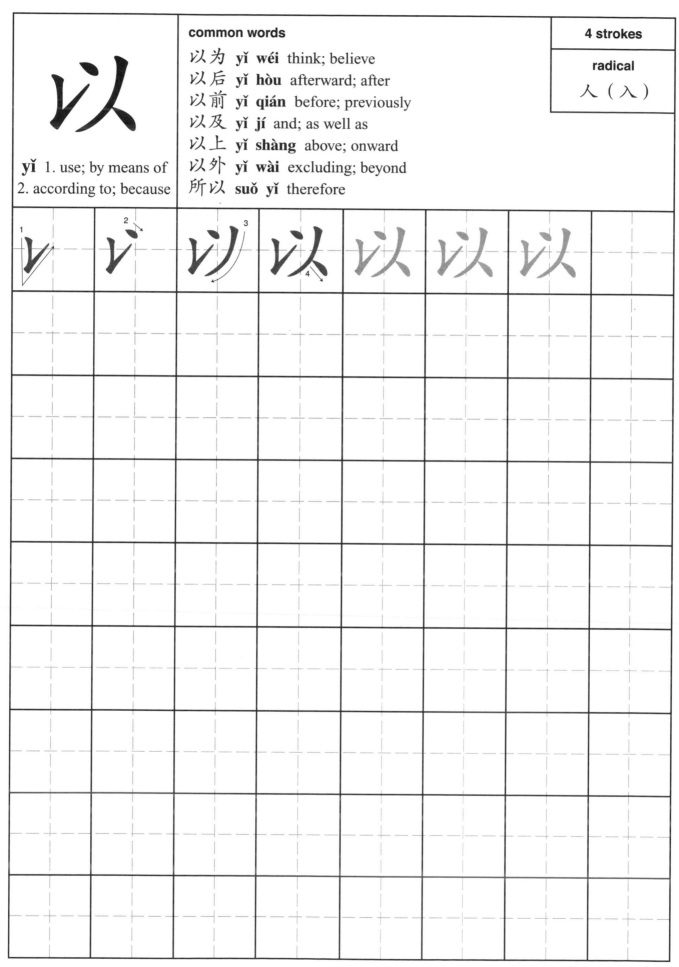

里

lǐ in; inside; within

common words

里面／里边／里头 **lǐ miàn/lǐ bian/lǐ tou** in; inside
家里 **jiā lǐ** in (one's) home/family
房里 **fáng lǐ** in the room
屋里 **wū lǐ** in the house
心里 **xīn lǐ** in the heart; mental state
邻里 **lín lǐ** neighborhood

7 strokes

radical

里

traditional form

裡

丨	冂	日	旦	甲	里	里	里
里	里					

外

wài 1. relatives of one's mother 2. outside

common words

外孙 **wài sūn** daughter's son
外婆 **wài pó** grandmother (maternal)
外人 **wài rén** outsider
外卖 **wài mài** take away (service)
门外 **mén wài** outside the gate/door
课外 **kè wài** extracurricular

5 strokes

radical
夕

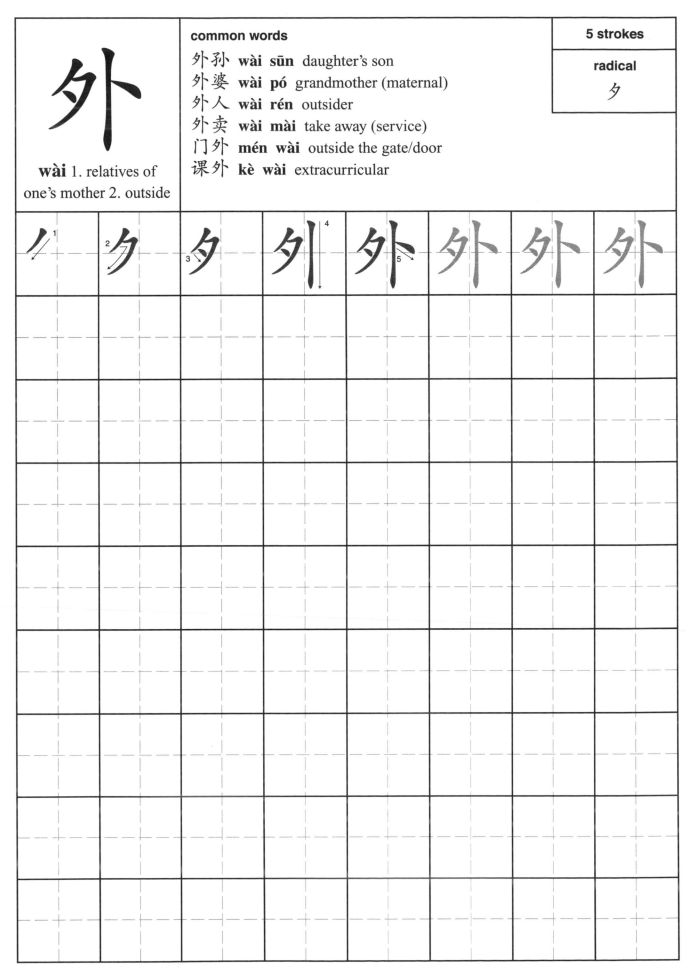

只

zhǐ only

radical

口

traditional form

祇

common words

只好／只得 **zhǐ hǒu/zhǐ dé** have to; must
只是 **zhǐ shì** only
只不过 **zhǐ bu guò** 1. only 2. but
只要 **zhǐ yào** so long as; provided that
只有 **zhǐ yǒu** only
不只 **bù zhǐ** not only; not just

丨	冂	口	只	只	只	只	只

想

xiǎng 1. think
2. reckon 3. want to

common words

想想看 **xiǎng xiǎng kàn** think about it
想起 **xiǎng qǐ** remember; recall
想要 **xiǎng yào** want to; wish for; feel like
想出／想到 **xiǎng chū/xiǎng dào** figure out; think of
想不到 **xiǎng bu dào** unexpected
猜想 **cāi xiǎng** guess; suppose

13 strokes

radical

心

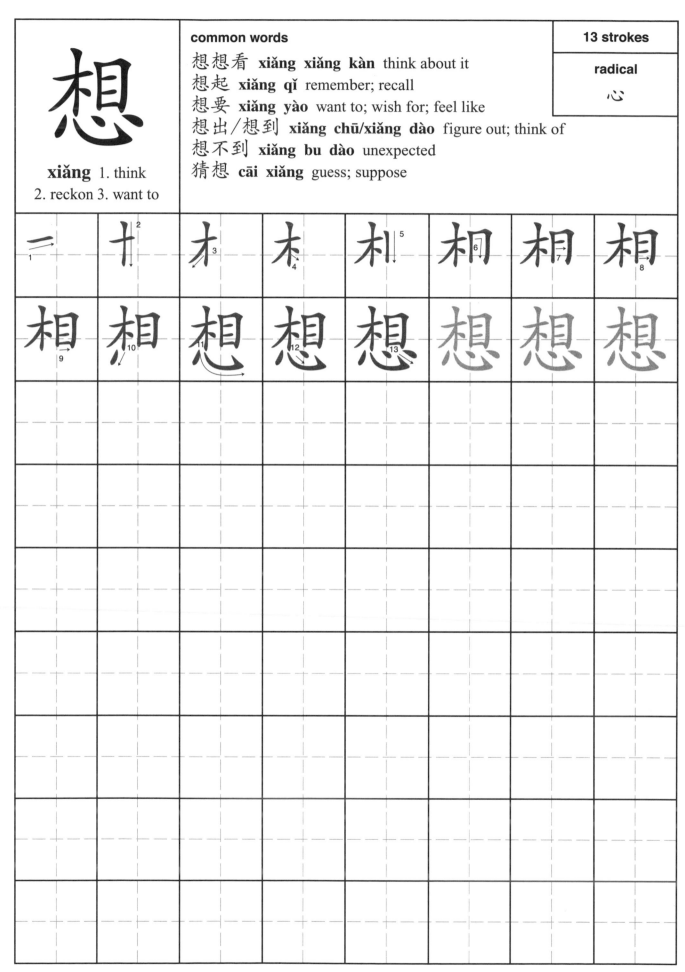

玩

wán play

common words

玩耍/游玩 **wán shuǎ/yóu wán** play

玩具 **wán jù** toy

玩弄 **wán nòng** 1. toy with 2. trick; flirt

开玩笑 **kāi wán xiào** (to) joke

好玩 **hào wán** love to play

好玩 **hǎo wán** fun; entertaining

radical

王

二₁	三₂	开₃	王₄	王₅	王₆	玩₇	玩₈
玩	玩	玩					

爱	**common words**	**10 strokes**
	爱好 **ài hào** hobby	
	爱心 **ài xīn** affection	**radical**
	爱上 **ài shàng** fall in love with	⌐ （爪）
	爱上网 **ài shàng wǎng** enjoy surfing (internet)	
	爱人 **ài ren** 1. spouse 2. lover	**traditional form**
ài 1. love 2. enjoy	可爱 **kě ài** cute; adorable	愛

⼆1	2 ⼃	爫 3	爫 4	爫 5	受	受 7	受 8
爱 9	爱 10	爱	爱	爱			

睡

shuì sleep

common words

睡醒 **shuì xǐng** wake up

睡衣 **shuì yī** pajamas

睡着 **shuì zháo** fall asleep

睡饱 **shuì bǎo** had a good sleep

想睡 **xiǎng shuì** feel like sleeping

打瞌睡 **dǎ kē shuì** dozing off

13 strokes

radical

目

觉	common words	9 strokes

jiào/jué 1. sleep 2. feel

common words

睡觉 **shuì jiào** sleep; go to bed
午觉 **wǔ jiào** afternoon nap
觉得 **jué de** feel
发觉 **fā jué** discover; realize
错觉 **cuò jué** illusion; misconception
不知不觉 **bù zhī bù jué** unconciously

radical

见

traditional form

覺

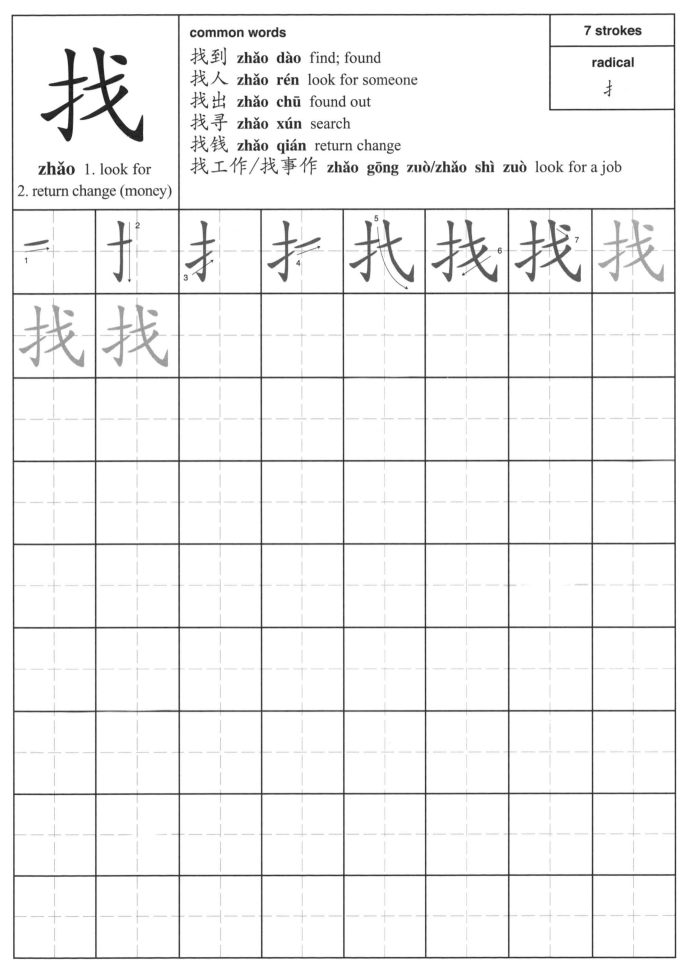

找

zhǎo 1. look for
2. return change (money)

common words

找到 **zhǎo dào** find; found
找人 **zhǎo rén** look for someone
找出 **zhǎo chū** found out
找寻 **zhǎo xún** search
找钱 **zhǎo qián** return change
找工作/找事作 **zhǎo gōng zuò/zhǎo shì zuò** look for a job

7 strokes

radical

扌

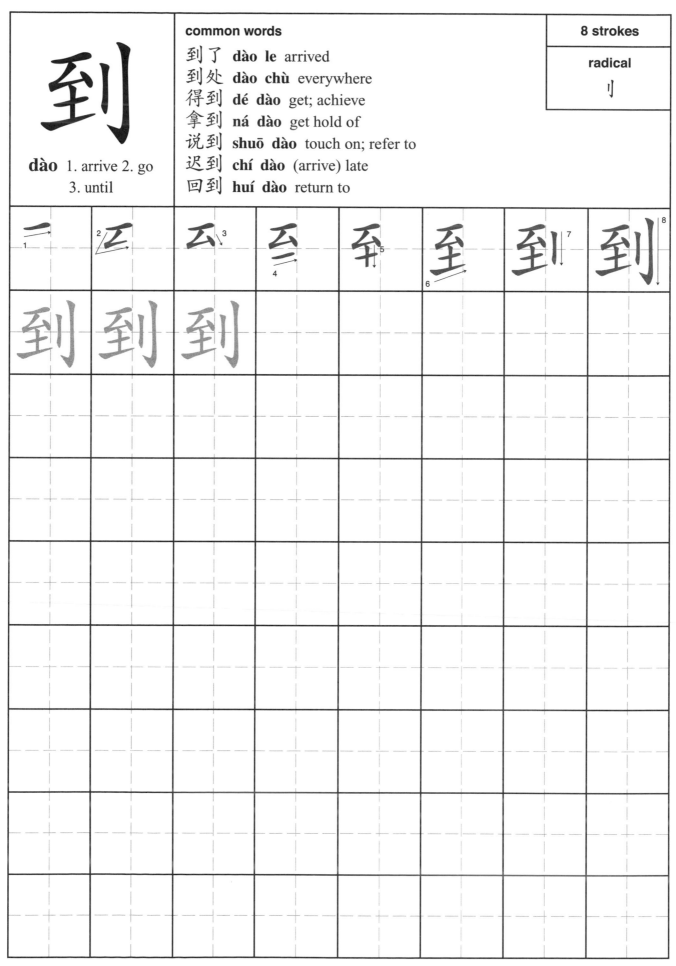

到

dào 1. arrive 2. go
3. until

common words

到了　**dào le**　arrived
到处　**dào chù**　everywhere
得到　**dé dào**　get; achieve
拿到　**ná dào**　get hold of
说到　**shuō dào**　touch on; refer to
迟到　**chí dào**　(arrive) late
回到　**huí dào**　return to

8 strokes

radical

刂

工

gōng 1. work
2. worker (in short)

common words

工人/员工 **gōng rén/yuán gōng** worker
工作 **gōng zuò** 1. (to) work 2. job; work
工具 **gōng jù** tool
工厂 **gōng chǎng** factory
工钱/工资 **gōng qian/gōng zī** pay; wage
停工 **tíng gōng** stop work
做工/打工 **zuò gōng/dǎ gōng** (to) work

3 strokes

radical

工

一　丁　工　工　工　工

作

zuò/zuō 1. do
2. write 3. feel

radical

亻

common words

作乐 **zuò lè** enjoy oneself
作弄 **zuō nòng** tease; make fun
作业 **zuò yè** homework; task
作家／作者 **zuò jiā/zuò zhě** composer; author
作客 **zuò kè** be a guest
合作 **hé zuò** cooperate
当作 **dāng zuò** regard as; consider to be

后		

hòu 1. back; behind
2. after; later

common words

后来/然后 **hòu lái/rán hòu** afterward; and then
后面/后边 **hòu miàn/hòu bian** back; behind
后门 **hòu mén** back door
后天 **hòu tiān** day after tomorrow
后父 **hòu fù** stepfather
今后 **jīn hòu** from now on
最后 **zuì hòu** 1. (the) last 2. finally; at last

6 strokes

radical
口

traditional form

後

一	厂	斤	后	后	后	后	后
后							

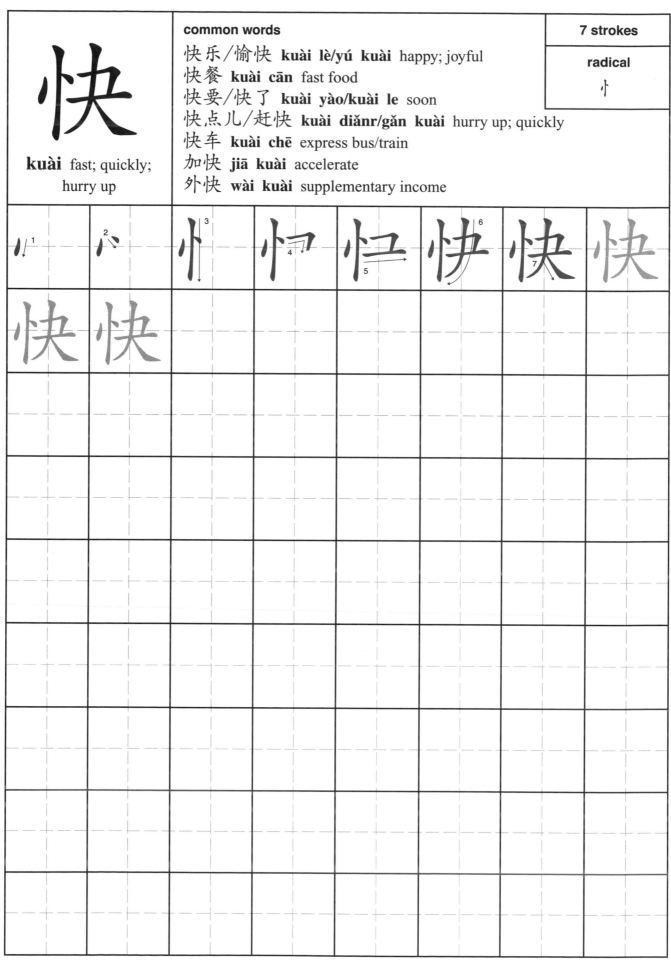

快

kuài fast; quickly;
hurry up

common words

快乐/愉快 **kuài lè/yú kuài** happy; joyful
快餐 **kuài cān** fast food
快要/快了 **kuài yào/kuài le** soon
快点儿/赶快 **kuài diǎnr/gǎn kuài** hurry up; quickly
快车 **kuài chē** express bus/train
加快 **jiā kuài** accelerate
外快 **wài kuài** supplementary income

7 strokes

radical

忄

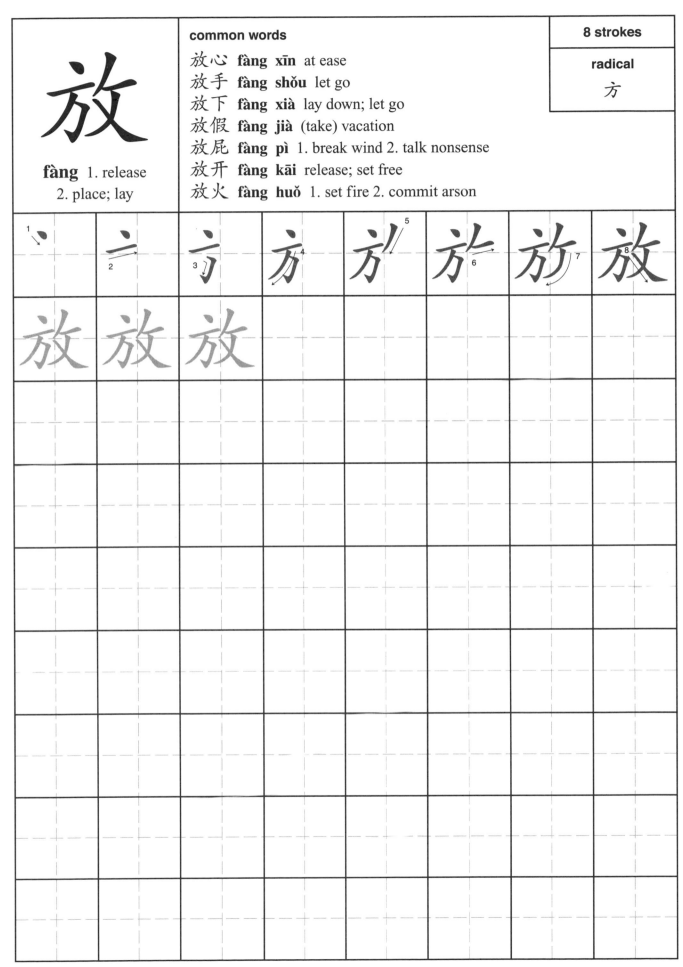

放

fàng 1. release
2. place; lay

common words

放心 **fàng xīn** at ease
放手 **fàng shǒu** let go
放下 **fàng xià** lay down; let go
放假 **fàng jià** (take) vacation
放屁 **fàng pì** 1. break wind 2. talk nonsense
放开 **fàng kāi** release; set free
放火 **fàng huǒ** 1. set fire 2. commit arson

8 strokes

radical

方

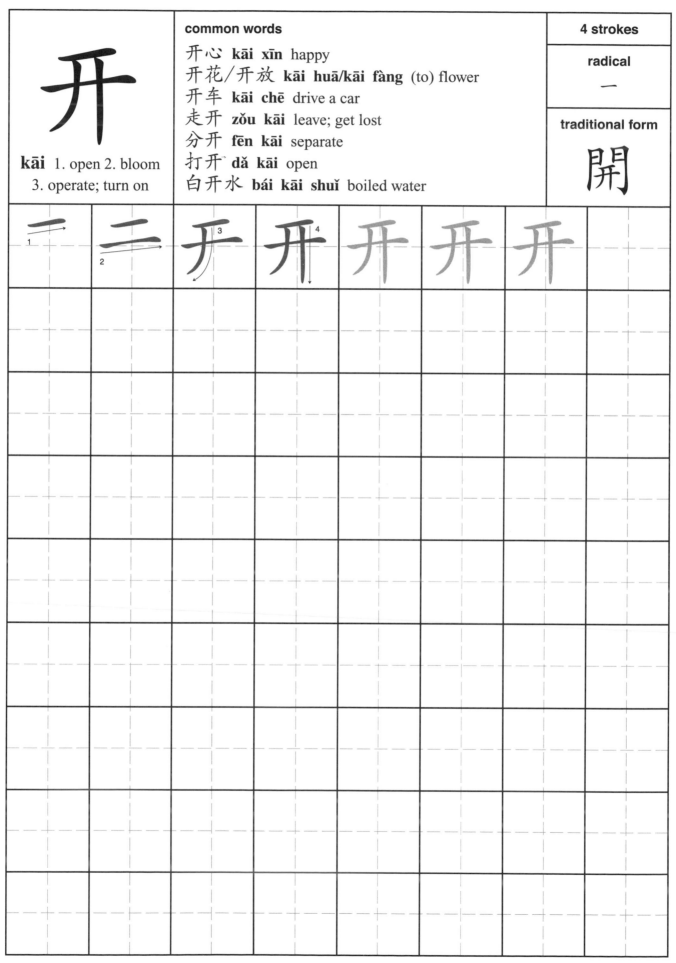

		common words		4 strokes

kāi 1. open 2. bloom
3. operate; turn on

common words

开心 **kāi xīn** happy
开花／开放 **kāi huā/kāi fàng** (to) flower
开车 **kāi chē** drive a car
走开 **zǒu kāi** leave; get lost
分开 **fēn kāi** separate
打开 **dǎ kāi** open
白开水 **bái kāi shuǐ** boiled water

4 strokes

radical
一

traditional form
開

意

yì 1. meaning 2. idea

common words

意见 **yì jiàn** opinion; view
意外 **yì wài** 1. accident 2. unexpected
注意 **zhù yì** pay attention; note
同意 **tóng yì** agree; accept
有意/故意 **yǒu yì/gù yì** purposely
大意 **dà yì** 1. careless 2. main meaning/idca
得意 **dé yì** complacent

13 strokes

radical

心

、	二	亠	立	立	音	音	音
音	音	意	意	意	意	意	意

思

sī think of; consider; ponder

common words

思想 **sī xiǎng** thinking; ideology
思考 **sī kǎo** think over; ponder
意思 **yì si** meaning
有意思 **yǒu yì si** interesting
没意思 **méi yì si** not interesting; meaningless
小意思 **xiǎo yì si** 1. That's easy! 2. small token
心思 **xīn si** 1. thinking 2. mood

9 strokes

radical

心

说

shuō speak

common words

说明 **shuō míng** explain
说话 **shuō huà** speak
说不定 **shuō bu dìng** perhaps; may be
说大话 **shuō dà huà** (to) boast
说谎 **shuō huǎng** (to) lie
爱说笑 **ài shuō xiào** love to joke
小说 **xiǎo shuō** novel

9 strokes

radical

讠

traditional form

說

丶	讠	讠	讠	讠	说	说	说
说	说	说	说				

空

kòng/kōng 1. sky
2. empty 3. free

common words

空白 **kòng bái** blank
空位 **kòng wèi** empty seat
空气 **kōng qì** air
空中 **kōng zhōng** mid-air
天空 **tiān kōng** sky
有空 **yǒu kòng** free

8 strokes

radical

穴

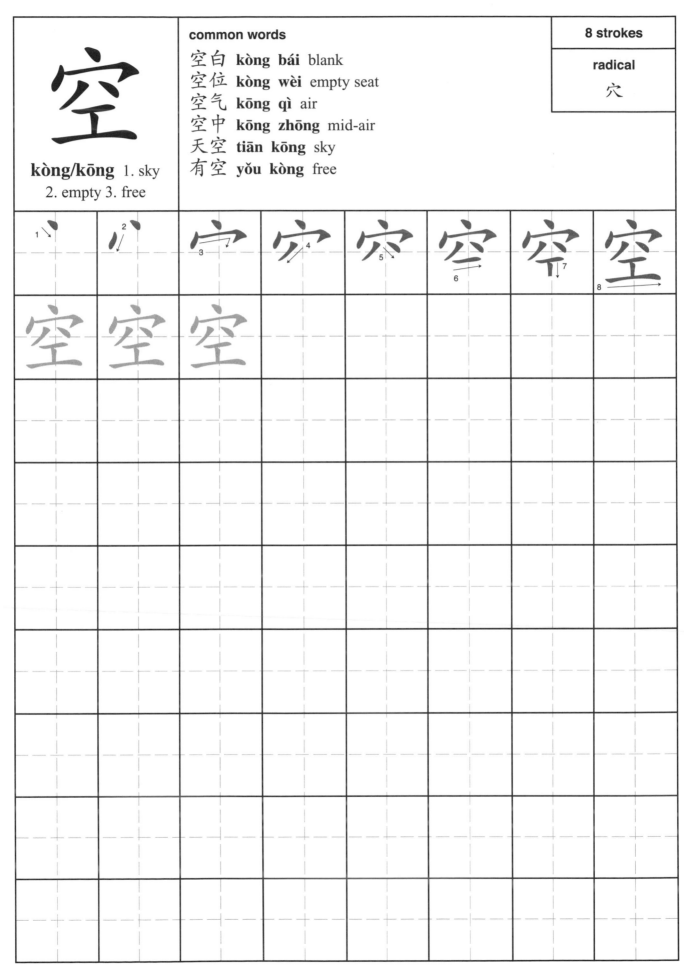

话

huà (one's) words

common words

话题 **huà tí** subject (of a conversation)
话剧 **huà jù** stage play
笑话 **xiào huà** joke
坏话 **huài huà** malicious talk
电话 **diàn huà** telephone
空话 **kōng huà** empty talk; idle talk

8 strokes

radical

讠

traditional form

話

丶	讠	讠	讠	讠	话	话	话
话	话	话					

要

yào/yāo 1. need
2. want 3. ask for

common words

要是 **yào shì** if
要好 **yào hǎo** on good terms, befriend
要求 **yāo qiú** request
要不／要不然 **yào bù/yào bu rán** otherwise; or else
要紧／重要 **yào jǐn/zhòng yào** important
就要 **jiù yào** about to
须要 **xū yào** need to

知

zhī know; knowledge

common words

知道 **zhī dào** know
知己 **zhī jǐ** bosom friend
明知 **míng zhī** know fully well
得知 **dé zhī** know/learn about
已知 **yǐ zhī** already known
通知／告知 **tōng zhī/gào zhī** notify; inform

8 strokes

radical

矢

道

dào 1. road; way
2. moral

common words

道歉 **dào qiàn** apologize
道谢 **dào xiè** (to) thank
道别 **dào bié** bid farewell; part
道理 **dào li** reasoning; doctrine
道路 **dào lù** road
味道 **wèi dào** taste; flavor
街道 **jiē dào** street

12 strokes

radical

辶

丶	⺍	丷	兰	芒	首	首	首
首	首	道	道	道	道	道	

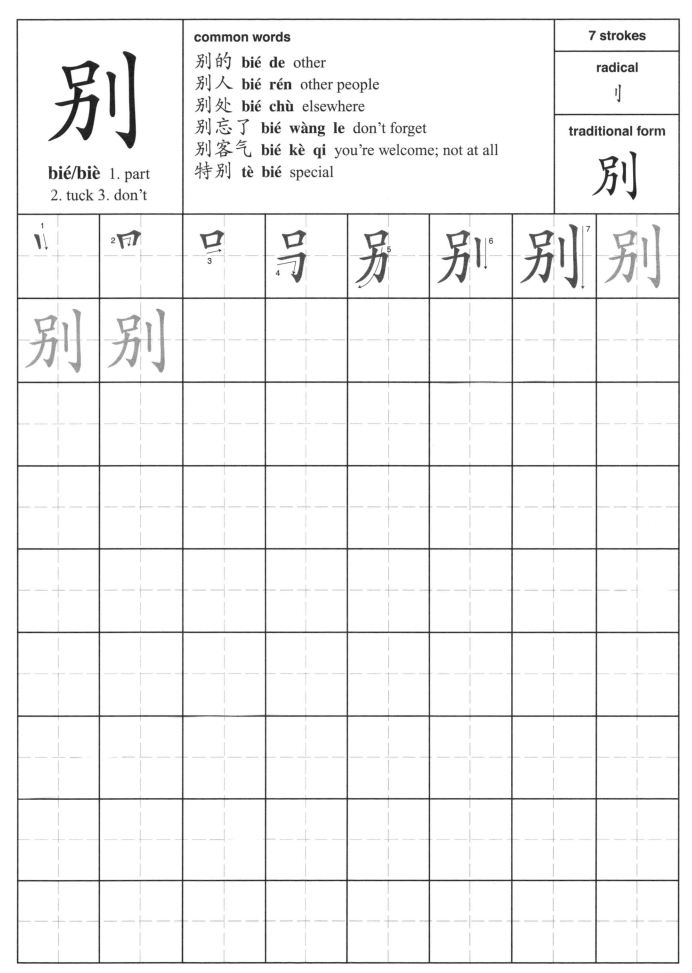

別

bié/biè 1. part
2. tuck 3. don't

common words

别的 **bié de** other
别人 **bié rén** other people
别处 **bié chù** elsewhere
别忘了 **bié wàng le** don't forget
别客气 **bié kè qi** you're welcome; not at all
特别 **tè bié** special

7 strokes

radical

刂

traditional form

別

客		**common words**				**9 strokes**
		客人 **kè rén** guest				**radical**
		客户 **kè hù** customer				宀
		客厅 **kè tīng** living room				
		客房 **kè fáng** guest room				
kè guest		客气 **kè qi** courteous; polite				
		常客 **cháng kè** regular customer				
		乘客 **chéng kè** passenger				

气

qì 1. gas 2. angry

common words

气死/气死人 **qì sǐ/qì sǐ rén** enraged
气味 **qì wèi** smell
气球 **qì qiú** balloon
气候 **qì hòu** weather
气力 **qì lì** strength
生气 **shēng qì** angry
小气 **xiǎo qì** 1. stingy; mean 2. in poor taste

4 strokes

radical

气

traditional form

氣

丿　气　气　气　气　气　气

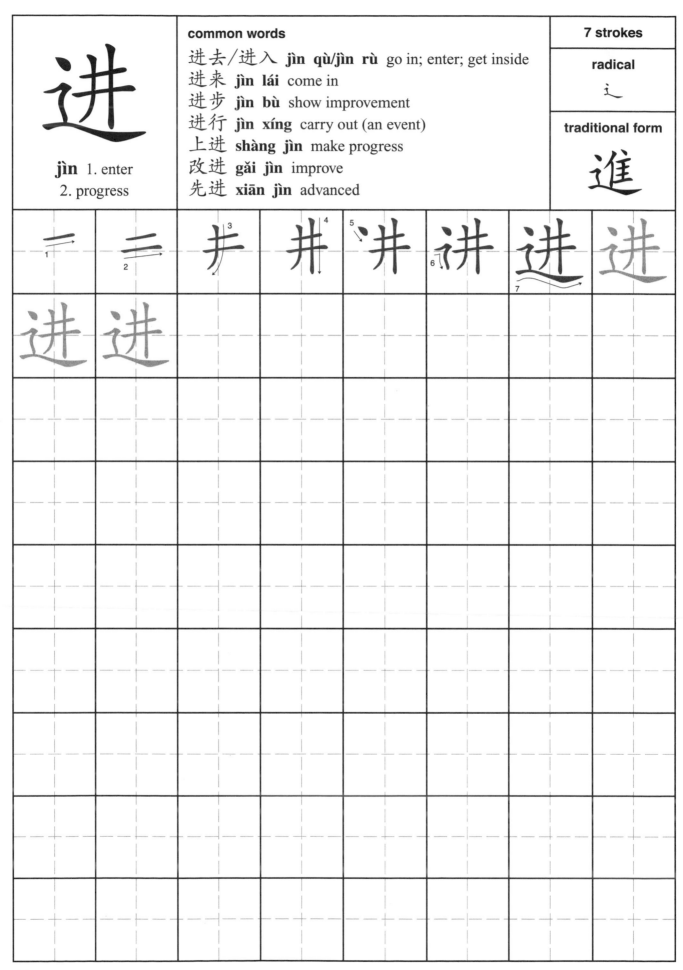

jìn 1. enter
2. progress

common words

进去/进入 **jìn qù/jìn rù** go in; enter; get inside
进来 **jìn lái** come in
进步 **jìn bù** show improvement
进行 **jìn xíng** carry out (an event)
上进 **shàng jìn** make progress
改进 **gǎi jìn** improve
先进 **xiān jìn** advanced

7 strokes

radical

辶

traditional form

進

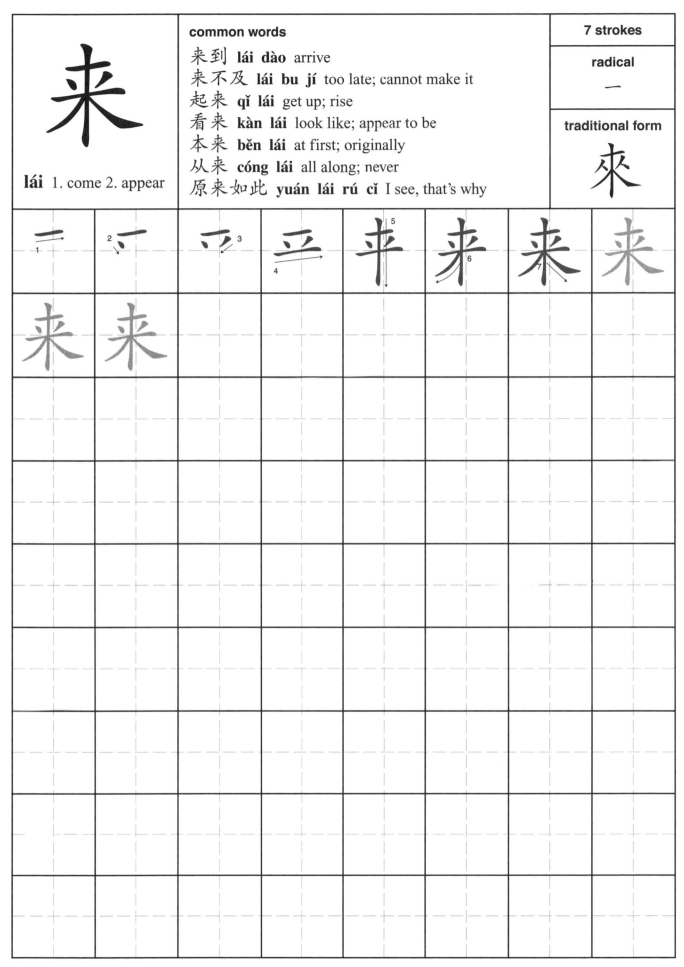

		common words	来到 **lái dào** arrive		7 strokes

来

lái 1. come 2. appear

common words

来到 **lái dào** arrive
来不及 **lái bu jí** too late; cannot make it
起来 **qǐ lái** get up; rise
看来 **kàn lái** look like; appear to be
本来 **běn lái** at first; originally
从来 **cóng lái** all along; never
原来如此 **yuán lái rú cǐ** I see, that's why

7 strokes

radical

一

traditional form

來

坐

zuò 1. sit 2. ride; travel by

radical

土

common words

坐下 **zuò xià** sit down
坐位 **zuò wèi** seat
坐牢 **zuò láo** imprison
坐飞机 **zuò fēi jī** travel by air/plane
坐船 **zuò chuán** travel by sea/boat
乘坐 **chéng zuò** travel by
静坐 **jìng zuò** sit in silence

呀

yā/ya 1. creeking
2. sentence-ending particle

common word

哎呀！/呀！ **aī yā/yā** Oh!; Ah! (expresses surprise, annoyance, reluctance, etc)

来呀！ **lái ya** Please come!

7 strokes

radical

口

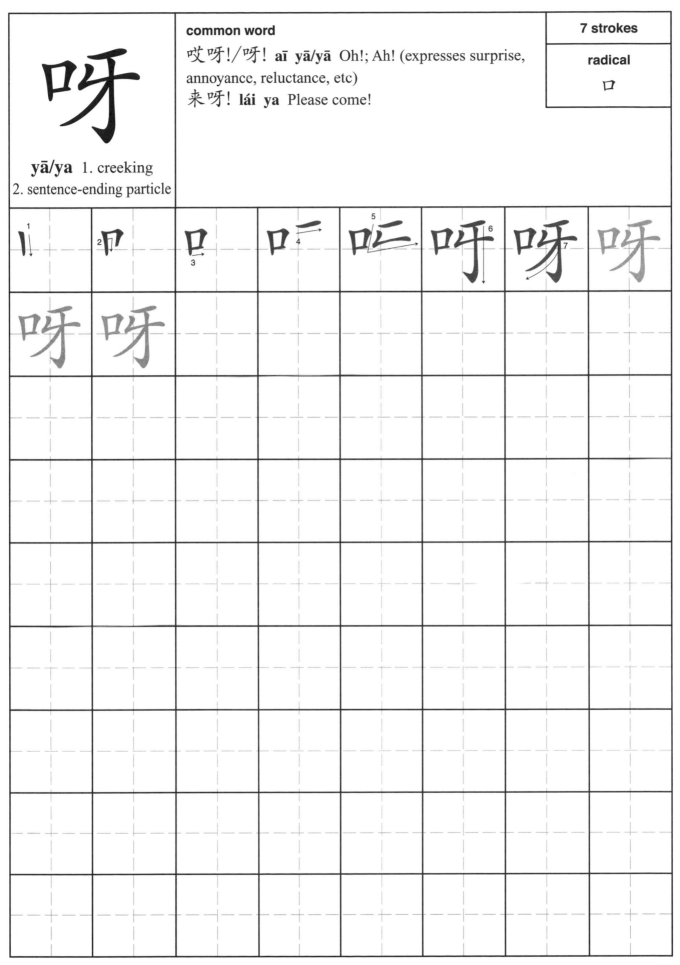

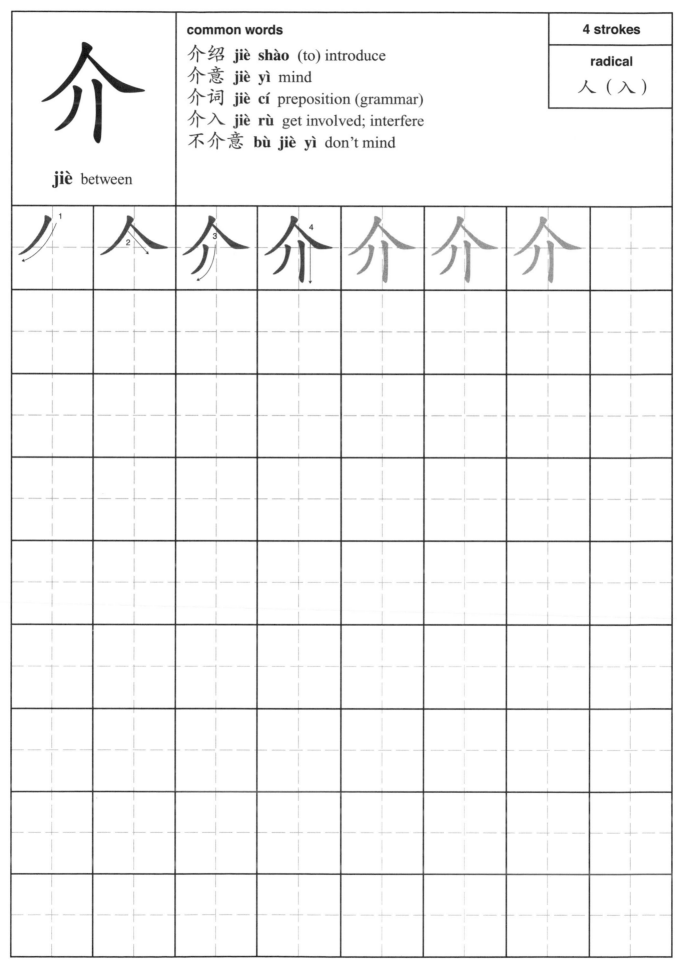

介

jiè between

common words

介绍 **jiè shào** (to) introduce
介意 **jiè yì** mind
介词 **jiè cí** preposition (grammar)
介入 **jiè rù** get involved; interfere
不介意 **bù jiè yì** don't mind

4 strokes

radical

人（入）

绍

shào join together;
connect

common words

介绍／绍介 **jiè shào/shào jiè** (to) introduce
介绍信 **jiè shào xìn** letter of introduction

8 strokes

radical

纟

traditional form

紹

纟	纟	纟	纠	纫	纫	绍	绍

绍	绍	绍					

高

gāo 1. tall; high
2. senior

radical

高

common words

高等 **gāo děng** high level
高大 **gāo dà** 1. huge 2. glorious
高矮 **gāo ǎi** height
高低 **gāo dī** 1. height 2. difference (in height/degree)
高地 **gāo dì** highland
高见 **gāo jiàn** opinion
高手 **gāo shǒu** expert

兴	**common words**	**6 strokes**

兴

xìng/xīng 1. prosper
2. excitement; happy

common words

兴趣 **xìng qù** interest
兴奋 **xīng fèn** excited
兴奋剂 **xīng fèn jì** stimulant
兴冲冲 **xīng chōng chōng** happily
高兴 **gāo xìng** happy
扫兴 **sǎo xīng** disappointed

6 strokes

radical

八（丷）

traditional form

興

漂

piāo/piǎo/piào
1. float; drift 2. rinse

common words

漂亮 **piào liang** beautiful; wonderful; outstanding
漂白 **piǎo bái** bleach
漂流 **piāo liú** drift
漂浮 **piāo fú** float

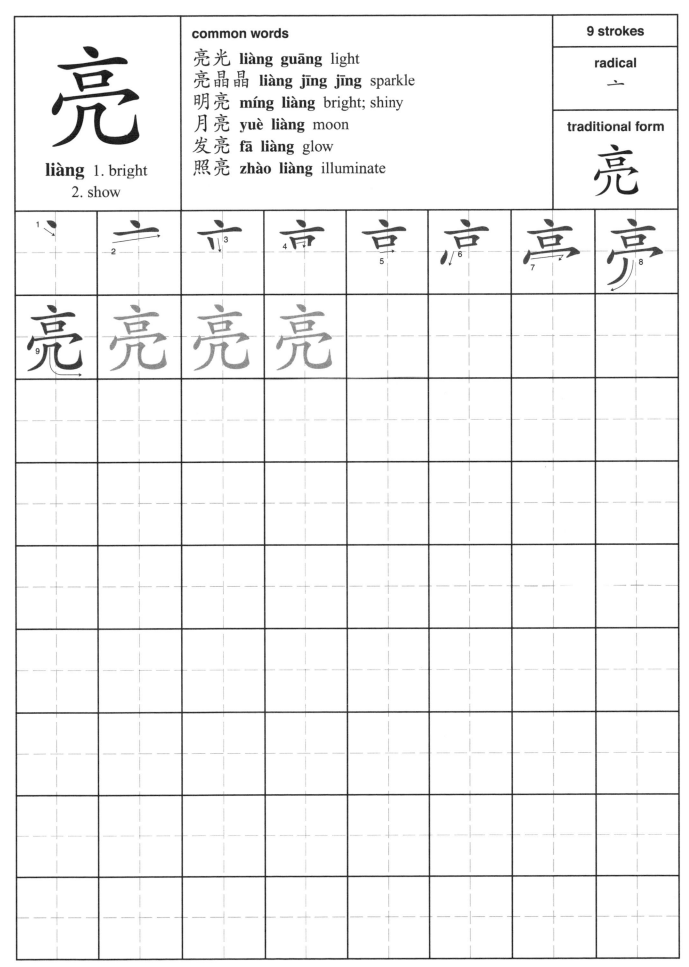

	common words	9 strokes

亮

liàng 1. bright
2. show

common words

亮光 **liàng guāng** light
亮晶晶 **liàng jīng jīng** sparkle
明亮 **míng liàng** bright; shiny
月亮 **yuè liàng** moon
发亮 **fā liàng** glow
照亮 **zhào liàng** illuminate

9 strokes

radical

亠

traditional form

亮

	common words	3 strokes

common words

口红 **kǒu hóng** lipstick
口袋 **kǒu dai** pocket
口气 **kǒu qì** tone (when saying something)
胃口 **wèi kǒu** 1. appetite 2. liking (in food)
门口 **mén kǒu** doorway
入口 **rù kǒu** entrance
窗口 **chuāng kǒu** window

kǒu 1. mouth
2. entrance; opening

3 strokes

radical
口

渴

kě 1. thirsty 2. eagerly

common words

渴求 **kě qiú** hunger for
渴望 **kě wàng** long for
口渴 **kǒu kě** thirsty
又渴又饿 **yòu kě yòu è** hungry and thirsty

12 strokes

radical

氵

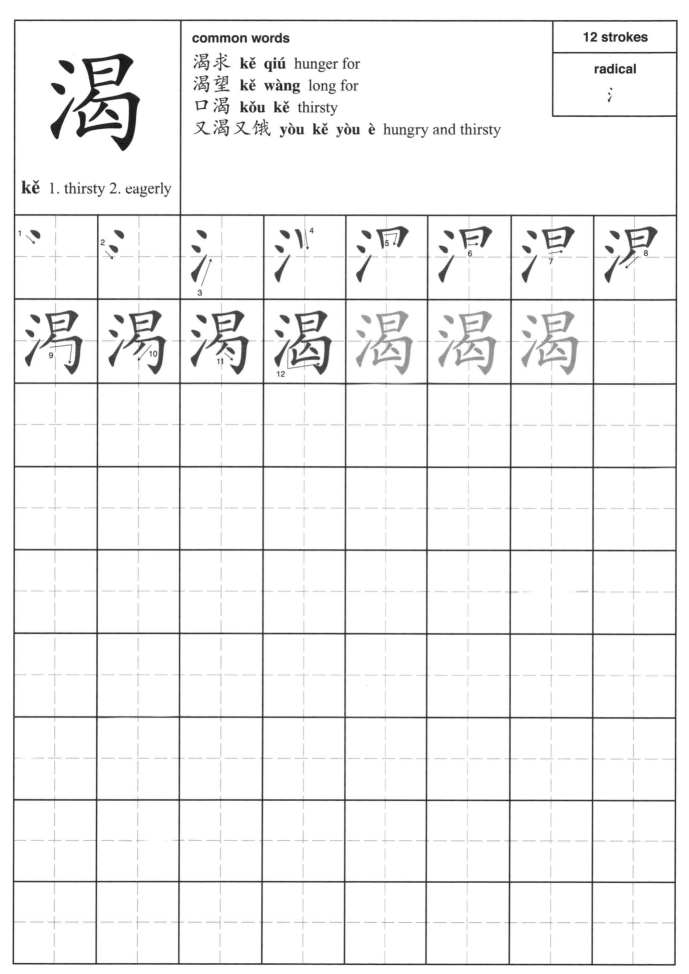

喝

hē/hè 1. drink
2. shout

common words

喝水 **hē shuǐ** drink water
喝茶 **hē chá** drink tea
喝酒 **hē jiǔ** drink alcohol
喝醉 **hē zuì** drunk
喝彩 **hè cǎi** applaud; cheer
请喝 **qǐng hē** please drink
好喝 **hǎo hē** taste good (drinks)

12 strokes

radical

口

茶

chá tea

common words

茶点 **chá diǎn** refreshments
茶叶 **chá yè** tea leaves
茶具 **chá jù** tea set
茶壶 **chá hú** teapot
泡茶 **pào chá** make tea
倒茶 **dào chá** pour tea
奶茶 **nǎi chá** milk tea

一	艹	艹	艹	艾	苓	苓	茶
茶	茶	茶	茶				

给

gěi 1. give 2. allow 3. for 4. ...to

common words

给以 **gěi yǐ** give
给忘了 **gěi wàng le** forgotten
送给 **sòng gěi** give as a present
卖给 **mài gěi** sell to
借给 **jiè gěi** lend to
嫁给 **jià gěi** marry to (a man)

9 strokes

radical

纟

traditional form

給

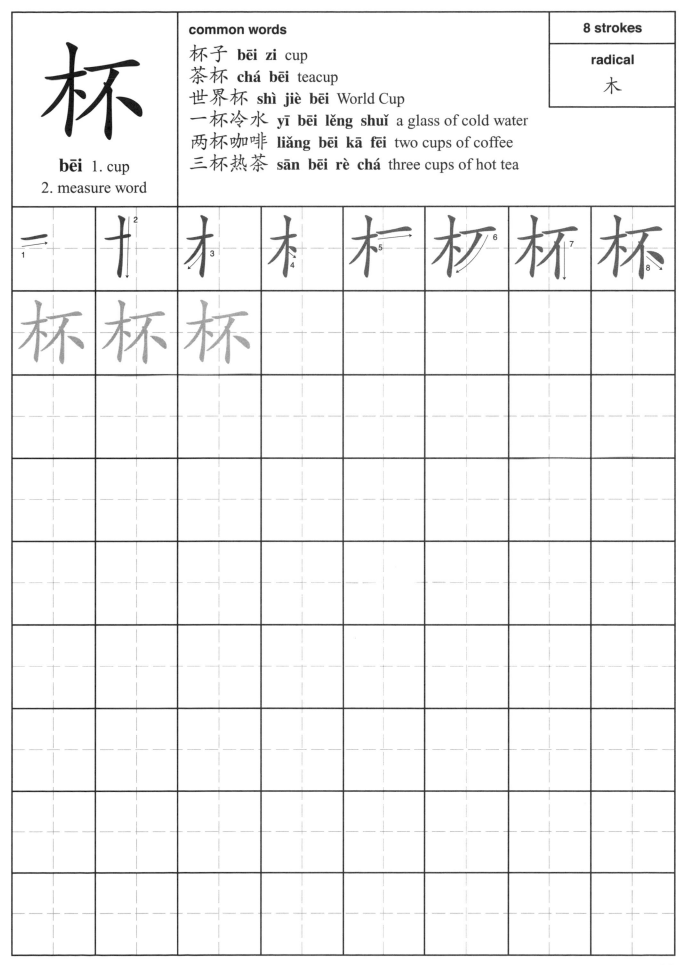

bēi 1. cup
2. measure word

common words

杯子 **bēi zi** cup
茶杯 **chá bēi** teacup
世界杯 **shì jiè bēi** World Cup
一杯冷水 **yī bēi lěng shuǐ** a glass of cold water
两杯咖啡 **liǎng bēi kā fēi** two cups of coffee
三杯热茶 **sān bēi rè chá** three cups of hot tea

8 strokes

radical

木

水

shuǐ 1. water 2. liquid

common words

水果 **shuǐ guǒ** fruit
水牛 **shuǐ niú** water buffalo
水池 **shuǐ chí** pond
汗水 **hàn shuǐ** sweat
汽水 **qì shuǐ** fizzy drink
薪水 **xīn shuǐ** salary
香水 **xiāng shuǐ** perfume

4 strokes

radical

水

丨 刁 水 水 水 水 水

100

就

jiù 1. and then; then
2. only

common words

就是 **jiù shì** 1. exactly 2. even (though) 3. only
就要 **jiù yào** about to
就算 **jiù suàn** even if
就读 **jiù dú** study
就任 **jiù rèn** take office
成就 **chéng jiù** achievement

12 strokes

radical
亠

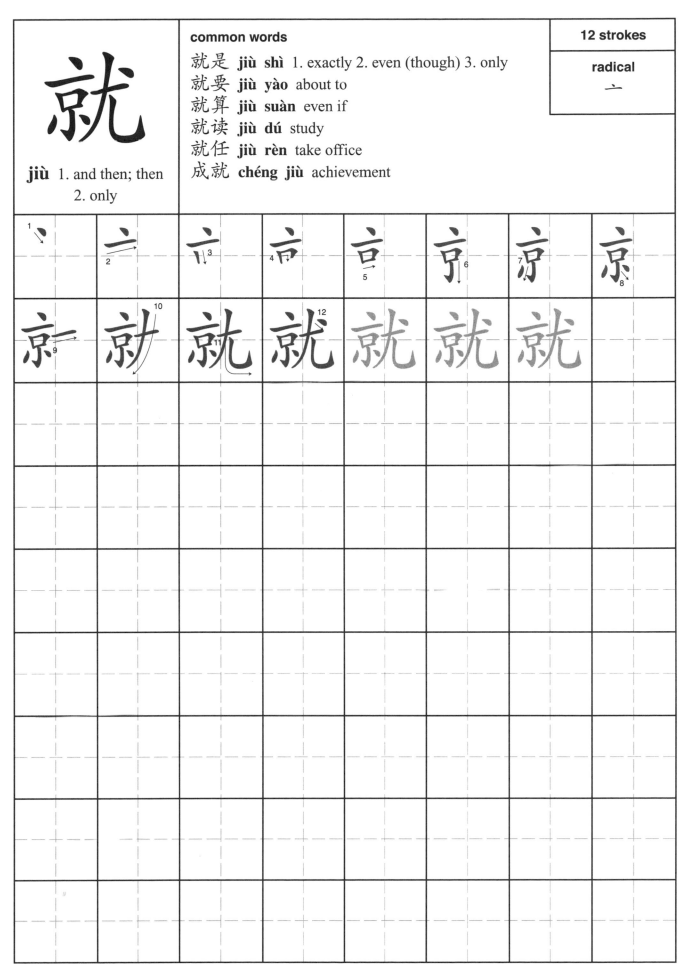

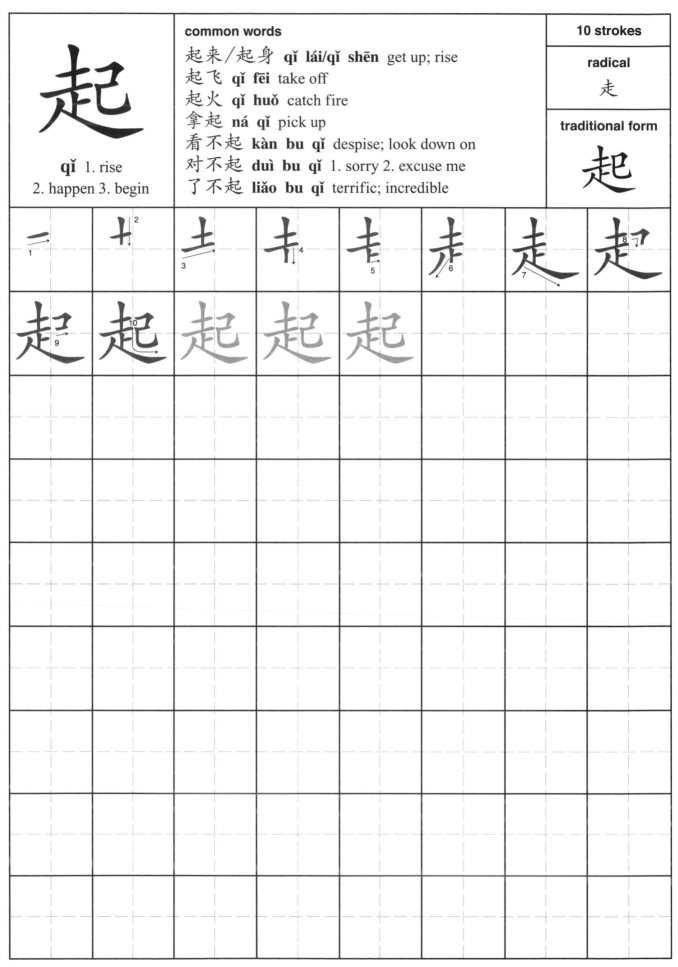

起

qǐ 1. rise
2. happen 3. begin

common words

起来/起身 **qǐ lái/qǐ shēn** get up; rise
起飞 **qǐ fēi** take off
起火 **qǐ huǒ** catch fire
拿起 **ná qǐ** pick up
看不起 **kàn bu qǐ** despise; look down on
对不起 **duì bu qǐ** 1. sorry 2. excuse me
了不起 **liǎo bu qǐ** terrific; incredible

10 strokes

radical

走

traditional form

起

床

chuáng 1. bed
2. measure word

common words

床单 **chuáng dān** bedsheet
床上 **chuáng shàng** on the bed
上床 **shàng chuáng** go to bed
起床 **qǐ chuáng** get out (of bed)
双人床 **shuāng rén chuáng** double bed
单人床 **dān rén chuáng** single bed
一床棉被 **yī chuáng mián bèi** a quilt

7 strokes

radical
广

traditional form
牀

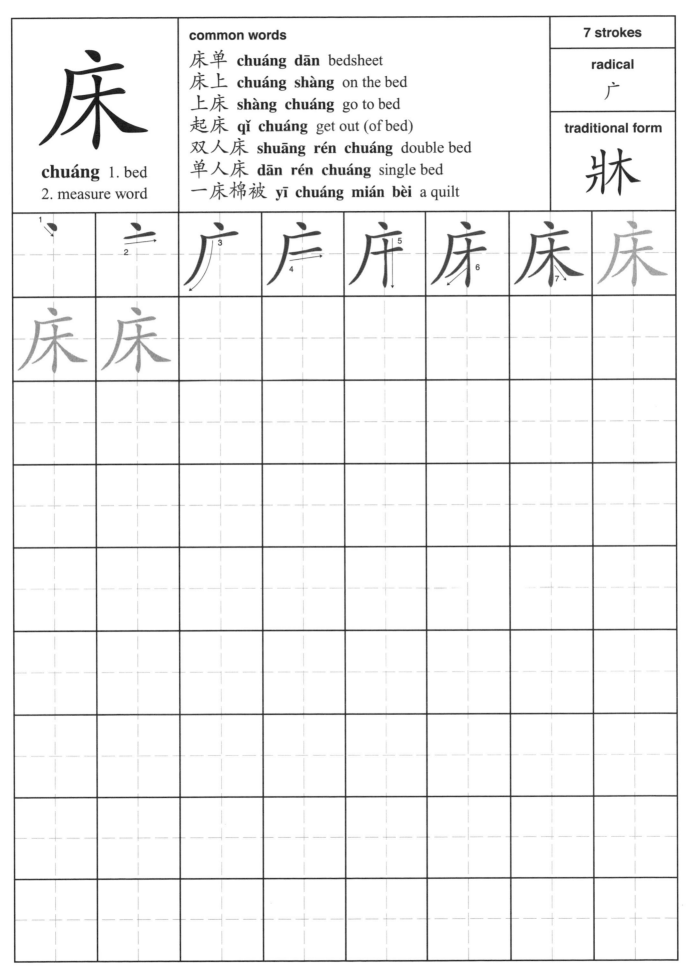

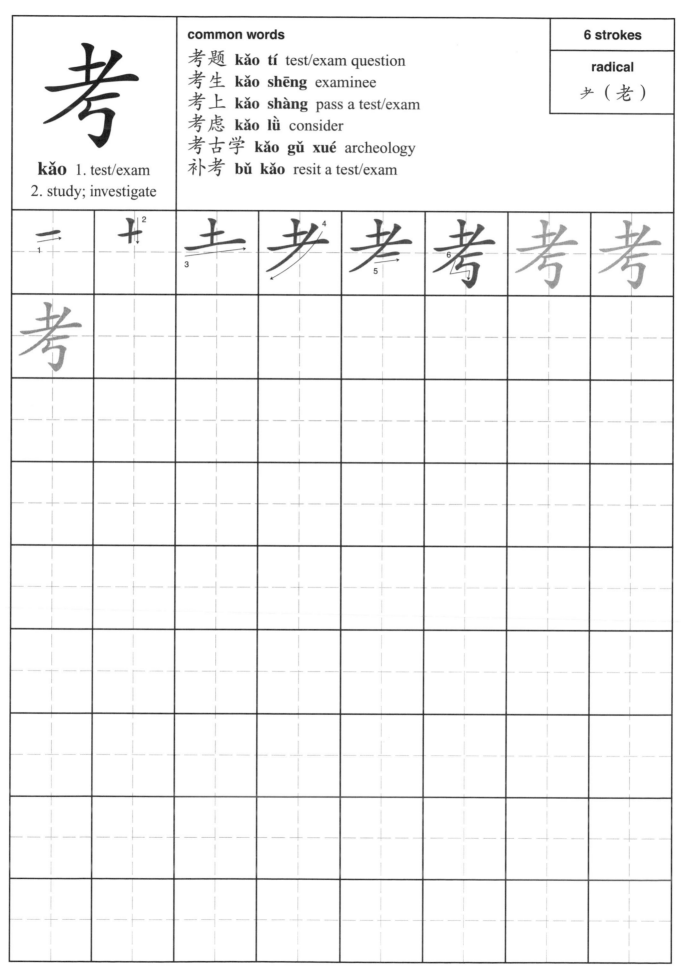

考

kǎo 1. test/exam
2. study; investigate

common words

考题 **kǎo tí** test/exam question
考生 **kǎo shēng** examinee
考上 **kǎo shàng** pass a test/exam
考虑 **kǎo lǜ** consider
考古学 **kǎo gǔ xué** archeology
补考 **bǔ kǎo** resit a test/exam

6 strokes

radical

耂（老）

	common words	8 strokes

试

shì 1. try; test
2. trial; experiment

common words

试试/试试看 **shì shì/shì shì kàn** try and see
试用 **shì yòng** try out
试验 **shì yàn** experiment
考试 **kǎo shì** test/exam
口试 **kǒu shì** oral exam
尝试 **cháng shì** try

8 strokes

radical

讠

traditional form

試

方

fāng 1. square (shape)
2. prescription

common words

方法 **fāng fǎ** method
方向 **fāng xiàng** direction
四方 **sì fāng** 1. square 2. all directions
西方 **xī fāng** west; western
大方 **dà fang** 1. generous 2. elegant
地方 **dì fāng** 1. place 2. part

4 strokes

radical

方

二　亡　方　方　方　方

便

biàn/pián 1. casual 2. then 3. excretion

common words

便饭 **biàn fàn** quick meal
便当 **biàn dāng** lunch box
便宜 **pián yi** cheap
方便 **fāng biàn** 1. convenient 2. appropriate 3. relieve oncself
以便 **yǐ biàn** in order to; so that
随便 **suí biàn** do as one likes; casual

9 strokes

radical

亻

帮

bāng 1. (to) help
2. measure word

common words

帮忙／帮助 **bāng máng/bāng zhù** (to) help; help
帮不上忙 **bāng bù shàng máng** unable to help
帮手 **bāng shǒu** assistant
帮凶 **bāng xiōng** accomplice
四帮人 **sì bāng rén** four gang of people

9 strokes

radical

巾

traditional form

幫

助

zhù (to) help; help

common words

助手／助理 **zhù shǒu/zhù lǐ** assistant
助词 **zhù cí** auxiliary word
帮助 **bāng zhù** (to) help; help
救助 **jiù zhù** relieve; help
赞助 **zàn zhù** sponsor
助人为乐 **zhù rén wéi lè** take pleasure in helping others

7 strokes

radical

力

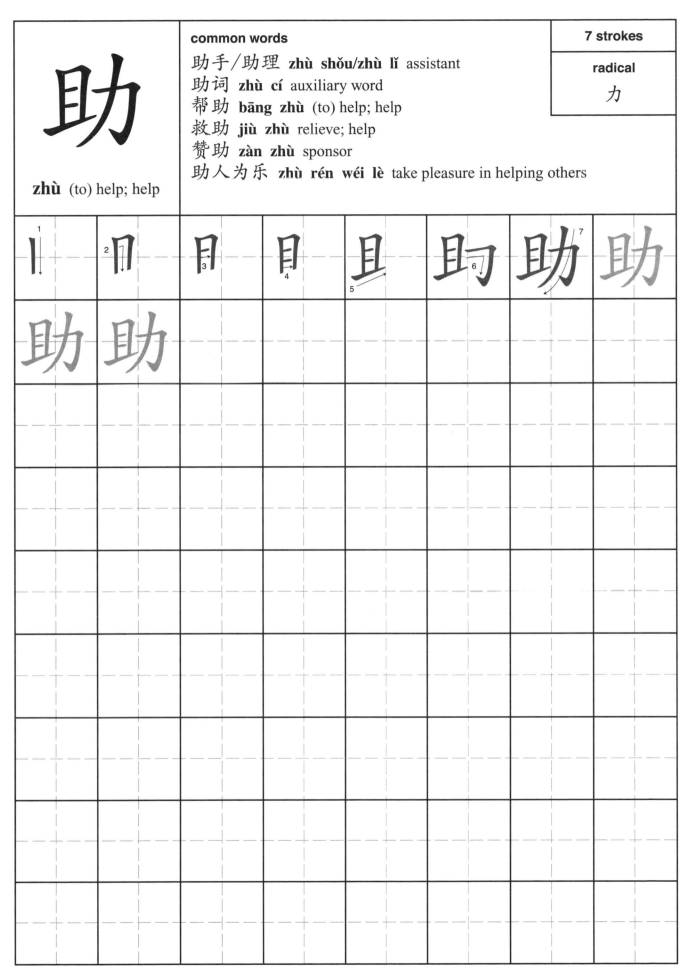

Hanyu Pinyin Index

Radical Index

[忄]
| 忙 | máng | 24 |
| 快 | kuài | 70 |

[宀]
| 客 | kè | 82 |

[辶]
还	hái/huán	25
道	dào	80
进	jìn	84

[纟]
| 绍 | shào | 89 |
| 给 | gěi | 98 |

4 strokes
[王]
现	xiàn	15
球	qiú	34
玩	wán	61

[木]
| 样 | yàng | 12 |
| 杯 | bēi | 99 |

[水]
| 水 | shuǐ | 100 |

[见]
| 觉 | jiào/jué | 64 |

[气]
| 气 | qì | 83 |

[斤]
| 所 | suǒ | 55 |

爫 [爪]
| 爱 | ài | 62 |

[欠]
| 歌 | gē | 42 |

[方]
| 方 | fāng | 106 |
| 放 | fàng | 71 |

[心]
怎	zěn	11
想	xiǎng	60
意	yì	73
思	sī	74

[礻]
| 视 | shì | 40 |

耂 [老]
| 考 | kǎo | 104 |

5 strokes
[目]
| 看 | kàn/kān | 35 |
| 睡 | shuì | 63 |

[钅]
| 钟 | zhōng | 20 |
| 错 | cuò | 51 |

[矢]
| 知 | zhī | 79 |

[穴]
| 空 | kòng/kōng | 76 |

6 strokes
覀 [西]
| 要 | yào/yāo | 78 |

[⺮]
| 等 | děng | 28 |

7 strokes
[走]
| 起 | qǐ | 102 |

足 [⻊]
| 跳 | tiào | 48 |

[里]
| 里 | lǐ | 57 |

9 strokes
[音]
| 音 | yīn | 45 |

10 strokes
[高]
| 高 | gāo | 90 |

English–Chinese Index

A

a quilt 一床棉被 yī chuáng mián bèi *103*
a glass of cold water 一杯冷水 yī bēi lěng shuǐ *99*
a little/a bit 一点儿/点儿 yī diǎnr/diǎnr *17*
a long time 半天 bàn tiān *18*; 好久 hǎo jiǔ *30*
ability 才能 cái néng *52*
able to 会 huì *47*
able to(?) 会不会(?) huì bu huì *47*
about to 就要 jiù yào *78, 101*
above 以上 yǐ shàng *56*
accelerate 加快 jiā kuài *70*
accent 口音 kǒu yīn *45*
accident 意外 yì wài *73*
accomplice 帮凶 bāng xiōng *108*
according to 以 yǐ *56*
achieve 得到 dé dào *66*
achievement 成就 chéng jiù *101*
acknowledge 公认 gōng rèn *13*
act as 为 wéi *22*
admit 认 rèn *13*
admit defeat 认输 rèn shū *13*
admit one's mistake 认错 rèn cuò *13*
adorable 可爱 kě ài *62*
advanced 先进 xiān jìn *84*
after 后 hòu *69*
affection 爱心 ài xīn *62*
after/afterward 以后 yǐ hòu *56*
afterward 后来/然后 hòu lái/rán hòu *69*
afternoon nap 午觉 wǔ jiào *64*
against 反对 fǎn duì *50*
age 岁数 suì shu *10*
agree/accept 同意 tóng yì *73*
Ah! 哎呀!/呀! āi yā/yà *87*
air 空气 kōng qì *76*
alike 一样/同样 yī yàng/tóng yàng *12*
all 所有 suǒ yǒu *55*
all along 从来 cóng lái *85*
all directions 四方 sì fāng *106*
all over the body 周身 zhōu shēn *31*
all right 还可以 hái kě yǐ *16*; 还好 hài hǎo *25*
all year round 常年 cháng nián *37*
allow 给 gěi *98*
already know 已知 yǐ zhī *79*
amount 分量 fèn liàng *19*
and 以及 yǐ jí *56*
...and so on 等等 děng děng *28*
and then 后来/然后 hòu lái/rán hòu *69*; 就 jiù *101*
angry 气/生气 qì/shēng qì *83*

B

babysit 看孩子 kān hái zi *35*
back 后/后面/后边 hòu/hòu miàn/hòu bian *69*
back door 后门 hòu mén *69*
ball 球 qiú *34*
ball (dance) 舞会 wǔ huì *49*
ball-shaped object 球 qiú *34*
ballet 芭蕾舞 bā lěi wǔ *49*
balloon 气球 qì qiú *83*
band 乐队 yuè duì *46*
bar top 吧台 bā tái *43*
basketball 蓝球 lán qiú *34*
bathroom 厕所 cè suǒ *55*
battery 电池 diàn chí *39*
be a guest 作客 zuò kè *68*
beat 跳 tiào *48*

(column 2, A continued)

anniversary 周年 zhōu nián *31*
answer 回答 huí dá *53*
apologize 道歉 dào qiàn *80*
appear 出现 chū xiàn *15*; 来 lái *85*
appear to be 看来 kàn lái *85*
appearance 样/样子 yàng/yàng zi *12*
appetite 胃口 wèi kǒu *94*
applaud 喝彩 hè cǎi *96*
appointment 约会 yuē huì *47*
appropriate 方便 fāng biàn *107*
approve 认同/认可 rèn tóng/rèn kě *13*
archeology 考古学 kǎo gǔ xué *104*
arrive 到 dào *66*; 来到 lái dào *85*
arrived 到了 dào le *66*
around 周/周围/四周 zhōu/zhōu wéi/sì zhōu *31*
as a result 因而 yīn ér *21*
as well as 以及 yǐ jí *56*
assistant 帮手 bāng shǒu *108*; 助手/助理 zhù shǒu/zhù lǐ *109*
ask/inquire 打听 dǎ tīng *44*
ask for 要 yào *78*
assemble 会合 huì hé *47*
at ease 放心 fàng xīn *71*
at first 本来 běn lái *85*
at last 最后 zuì hòu *69*
at present 现在 xiàn zài *15*
at the end 末了 mò liǎo *32*
audience 听众 tīng zhòng *44*
author 作家/作者 zuò jiā/zuò zhě *68*
auxiliary word 助词 zhù cí *109*

film/movie 电影 diàn yǐng *39*
finally 最后 zuì hòu *69*
find/found 找到 zhǎo dào *65*
Fine! 好吧 hǎo ba *43*
first birthday 周岁 zhōu suì *10*
five minutes (time) 五分/五分钟 wǔ fēn/wǔ fēn zhōng *19*
five points/marks 五分 wǔ fēn *19*
fizzy drink 汽水 qì shuǐ *100*
flavor 味道 wèi dào *80*
flirt 玩弄 wán nòng *61*
float 漂/漂浮 piāo/piāo fú *92*
(to) flower 开花/开放 kāi huā/kāi fàng *72*
fond of 喜/喜欢/喜爱 xǐ/xǐ huān/xǐ ài *26*
football 足球 zú qiú *34*
for 为/为了 wéi/wèi le *22*; 给 gěi *98*
for a long time 久/长久 jiǔ/cháng jiǔ *30*
for a very long time 久久 jiǔ jiǔ *30*
forever 永久 yǒng jiǔ *30*
forgotten 给忘了 gěi wàng le *98*
found out 找出 zhǎo chū *65*
four gang of people 四帮人 sì bāng rén *108*
free 空/有空 kòng/yǒu kòng *76*
frequently 常常/时常 cháng cháng/shí cháng *37*
from now on 今后 jīn hòu *69*
fruit 水果 shuǐ guǒ *100*
fun 好玩 hǎo wán *61*
funny 可笑 kě xiào *16*
furthermore 还有 hái yǒu *25*

G

gas 气 qì *83*
general knowledge 常识 cháng shí *14*
generous 大方 dà fang *106*
genius 天才 tiān cái *52*
get 得到 dé dào *66*
get hold of 拿到 ná dào *66*
get inside 进去/进入 jìn qù/jìn rù *84*
get involved 介入 jiè rù *88*
get lost 走开 zǒu kāi *72*
get out (of bed) 起床 qǐ chuáng *103*
get rid of/remove 去 qù *54*
get up 起来 qǐ lái *85*
give 给/给以 gěi/gěi yǐ *98*
give as a present 送给 sòng gěi *98*
glorious 高大 gāo dà *90*
glow 发亮 fā liàng *93*
go for a movie 看电影 kàn diàn yǐng *35*
go 到 dào *66*

go back 回去 huí qù *54*
go in 进去/进入 jìn qù/jìn rù *84*
go out 出去 chū qù *54*
go to 去 qù *54*
go to bed 睡觉 shuì jiào *64*; 上床 shàng chuáng *103*
grade/rank 等 děng *28*
grandmother (maternal) 外婆 wài pó *58*
guess 猜想 cāi xiǎng *60*
guest 客/客人 kè/kè rén *82*
guest room 客房 kè fáng *82*

H

had a good sleep 睡饱 shuì bǎo *63*
had better 还是 hái shi *25*
half 半 bàn *18*
half day 半天 bàn tiān *18*
half past nine 九点半 jiǔ diǎn bàn *18*
happen 起 qǐ *102*
happily 兴冲冲 xīng chōng chōng *91*
happy 喜 xǐ *26*; 欢 huān *27*; 乐 lè *46*; 快乐/愉快 kuài lè/yú kuài *70*
happy 欢喜 huān xǐ *27*; 欢乐 huān lè *27, 46*; 开心 kāi xīn *72*; 兴/高兴 xìng/gāo xìng *91*
happy event 喜事 xǐ shì *26*
hastily 急忙 jí máng *24*
have a look 看看 kàn kan *35*
have to 只好/只得 zhǐ hǎo/zhǐ dé *59*
hear 听 tīng *44*
heard 听见/听到 tīng jiàn/tīng dào *44*
heart palpitation/heartbeat 心跳 xīn tiào *48*
heartening 可喜 kě xǐ *26*
height 高矮/高低 gāo ǎi/gāo dī *90*
(to) help 帮 bāng *108*
(to) help/help 帮忙 bāng máng *24, 108*; 帮助 bāng zhù *108, 109*; 助 zhù *109*
high 高 gāo *90*
high class 上等 shàng děng *28*
high jump 跳高 tiào gāo *48*
high level 高等 gāo děng *90*
highland 高地 gāo dì *90*
hobby 爱好 ài hào *62*
hold a meeting 开会 kāi huì *47*
homework 作业 zuò yè *68*
hour (time) 钟头 zhōng tóu *20*
how(?) 怎/怎么(?) zěn/zěn me *11*
how about it(?) 怎样(?)/怎么样(?) zěn yàng/zěn me yàng *11*
how old(?) 几岁(?) jǐ suì *10*
huge 高大 gāo dà *90*

List of Radicals

— 1 stroke —

1 、 dot
2 一 one
3 ∣ down
4 丿 left
5 ⌐ "back-turned stroke"
6 ⌐ "top of 刁"
7 乙 twist

— 2 strokes —

8 冫 ice
9 亠 lid
10 讠 (side-) words
11 二 two
12 十 ten
13 厂 slope
14 ナ "top of 左"
15 匚 basket
16 卜 (上) divine
17 刂 (side) knife
18 冖 crown
19 冂 borders
20 ⺈ "top of 每"
21 亻 (side-)man
22 厂 "top of 后"
23 人 (入) person (enter)
24 八 (丷) eight
25 乂 "bottom of 义"
26 勹 wrap
27 刀 (⺈) knife
28 力 strength
29 儿 son
30 几 (几) table
31 マ "top of 予"
32 卩 seal
33 阝 (on the left) mound
34 阝 (on the right) city
35 又 right hand
36 ⻊ march
37 厶 cocoon
38 凵 bowl
39 匕 ladle

— 3 strokes —

40 氵 "three-dots water"
41 忄 (side-) heart
42 爿 bed
43 亡 to flee
44 广 lean-to
45 宀 roof
46 门 gate
47 辶 halt
48 工 work
49 土 (士) earth (knight)
50 艹 grass
51 廾 clasp
52 大 big
53 尢 lame
54 寸 thumb
55 扌 (side-) hand
56 弋 dart
57 巾 cloth

58 口 mouth
59 囗 surround
60 山 mountain
61 屮 sprout
62 彳 step
63 彡 streaks
64 夕 dusk
65 夂 follow, slow
66 丸 bullet
67 尸 corpse
68 饣 (side-) food
69 犭 (side-) dog
70 彐 (彑,彐) pig's head
71 弓 bow
72 己 (巳) self
73 女 woman
74 子 (孑) child
75 马 horse
76 幺 coil
77 纟 (糸) silk
78 巛 river
79 小 (⺌) small

— 4 strokes —

80 灬 "fire-dots"
81 心 heart
82 斗 peck
83 火 fire
84 文 pattern
85 方 square
86 户 door
87 礻 (side-) sign
88 王 king
89 ⺞ "top of 青"
90 天 (夭) heaven (tender)
91 韦 walk off
92 耂 "top of 老"
93 甘 twenty
94 木 tree
95 不 not
96 犬 dog
97 歹 chip
98 瓦 tile
99 牙 tooth
100 车 car
101 戈 lance
102 止 toe
103 日 sun
104 曰 say
105 中 middle
106 贝 cowrie
107 见 see
108 父 father
109 气 breath
110 牛 cow
111 手 hand
112 毛 fur
113 攵 knock
114 片 slice
115 斤 ax
116 爪 (爫) claws
117 尺 foot (length)
118 月 moon/meat

119 殳 club
120 欠 yawn
121 风 wind
122 氏 clan
123 比 compare
124 聿 "top of 書"
125 水 water

— 5 strokes —

126 立 stand
127 疒 sick
128 穴 cave
129 衤 (side-) gown
130 夫 "top of 春"
131 玉 jade
132 示 sign
133 去 go
134 ⺍ "top of 劳"
135 甘 sweet
136 石 rock
137 龙 dragon
138 戊 halberd
139 ⺍ "top of 常"
140 业 business
141 目 eye
142 田 field
143 由 from
144 申 stretch
145 罒 net
146 皿 dish
147 钅 (side-) gold
148 矢 arrow
149 禾 grain
150 白 white
151 瓜 melon
152 鸟 bird
153 皮 skin
154 ⺪ back
155 矛 spear
156 疋 bolt

— 6 strokes —

157 羊 (羋,羌) sheep
158 夹 roll
159 米 rice
160 齐 line-up
161 衣 gown
162 亦 (亦) also
163 耳 ear
164 臣 bureaucrat
165 戋 "top of 裁"
166 西 (覀) cover (west)
167 束 thorn
168 亚 inferior
169 而 beard
170 页 head
171 至 reach
172 光 light
173 虍 tiger
174 虫 bug
175 缶 crock
176 耒 plow
177 舌 tongue

178 竹 (⺮) bamboo
179 臼 mortar
180 自 small nose
181 血 blood
182 舟 boat
183 羽 wings
184 艮 (⺕) stubborn

— 7 strokes —

185 言 words
186 辛 bitter
187 辰 early
188 麦 wheat
189 走 walk
190 赤 red
191 豆 flask
192 束 bundle
193 酉 wine
194 豕 pig
195 里 village
196 足 (⻊) foot
197 采 cull
198 豸 snake
199 谷 valley
200 身 torso
201 角 horn

— 8 strokes —

202 青 green
203 卓 "side of 朝"
204 雨 rain
205 非 wrong
206 齿 teeth
207 黾 toad
208 隹 dove
209 金 gold
210 鱼 fish

— 9 strokes —

211 音 tone
212 革 hide
213 是 be
214 骨 bone
215 香 scent
216 鬼 ghost
217 食 food

— 10 strokes —

218 高 tall
219 鬲 cauldron
220 彡 hair

— 11 strokes —

221 麻 hemp
222 鹿 deer

— 12 strokes —

223 黑 black

— 13 strokes —

224 鼓 drum
225 鼠 mouse
226 鼻 big nose